"Think of this book as Jeff Foxworthy meets Donald Trump. You get all of The Donald's wisdom dished up in some of the most hilarious business adventures ever described anywhere. Only Tim would learn a major business lesson from having his daddy try to electrocute him. If it ain't fun, don't do it. By that advice, you should read this book—it's an entrepreneur's gold mine nestled in a silly foam container."

—Jerry Newman
Author, *My Secret Life on the McJob*

Everything
I Know About Business
I Learned from My Mama

A Down-Home Approach
to Business and Personal Success

TIM KNOX

John Wiley & Sons, Inc.

Published by John Wiley & Sons, Inc., Hoboken, New Jersey
Published simultaneously in Canada

Wiley Bicentennial Logo: Richard J. Pacifico

For general information on our other products and services or for technical support, please contact our Customer Care Department within the United States at (800) 762-2974, outside the United States at (317) 572-3993 or fax (317) 572-4002.

Wiley also publishes its books in a variety of electronic formats. Some content that appears in print may not be available in electronic books. For more information about Wiley products, visit our web site at www.wiley.com.

Library of Congress Cataloging-in-Publication Data:

Knox, Tim, 1960–
    Everything I know about business I learned from my mama : a down-home
approach to business and personal success / Tim Knox.
        p.   cm.
    ISBN 978-0-470-12756-8
    1. Success in business.   2. Success.   3. Industrial management.   4.
Entrepreneurship.   I. Title.
HF5386.K753 2007
650.1—dc22

                                                    2006101142

Printed in the United States of America.

10   9   8   7   6   5   4   3   2   1

CONTENTS

CONTENTS

CONTENTS

"Business is like extreme skiing. The person who wins is the one who screws up the least and doesn't die."

—Bo Peabody

"Don't worry about people stealing your ideas. If your ideas are any good, you'll have to ram them down people's throats."

—Howard Aiken

"My son is now an 'entrepreneur.' That's what you're called when you don't have a job."

—Ted Turner

"And everything is possible; you've just got to find a way to make it work."

—Wally Amos

FOREWORD

The workplace is changing dramatically. Experts tell us we are rapidly moving toward a workplace where only 50 percent of American workers are employees. The rest of us are going to be consultants, temps, contingency workers, independent contractors, entrepreneurs, and other creative titles as we scramble to keep up with the new opportunities appearing. Scott Adams of *Dilbert* fame says "Frightened Chipmunk" would be an appropriate title in this volatile work environment—but that doesn't look very impressive on a business card.

I first met Tim Knox at a writer's conference where we were both looking to refine and enhance our writing efforts. His unique and brilliant thinking, combined with his ready wit and humor, had me engaged and asking for more immediately. His hilarious slant on business drew me in, but I also saw the depth of his business understanding. I learned from his history that although he grew up without many advantages, he placed no blame and not only accepted but welcomed taking responsibility for his current position. The lessons learned from starting with nothing, attempting to climb the corporate ladder, and enduring the inevitable bloody noses from self-owned business make Tim the perfect candidate to share hope, encouragement, and inspiration with those struggling with the changing workplace. Not only does he have valuable knowledge to share; his desire is to be a world changer and share that expertise freely.

Every now and then I find a book that is so inspiring I immediately start making a list of all the people I know who *must* have a copy. *Everything I Know About Business I Learned from My Mama* is one of those books. As a career coach, I encounter people every day who are terrified by the often unexpected and unwelcome changes in traditional employment. *Everything I Know About Business I Learned from My Mama* offers hope—not the kind of empty hope that would have you close your eyes and trust that things are not really changing. No, it offers the kind of real hope that shows the way to take advantage of the changes, rather than feeling victimized by them.

In his engaging style, Tim shows how to live an intentional life, how to *decide* to be a success and then how to experience true success in multiple areas of your life. He describes how "thinking too much" got him fired and yet is probably his greatest asset—and why it can be yours as well. His funny stories of growing up in Alabama will convince you that opportunity does not knock; you have to go looking for it. He proposes real solutions and new work models that are available to all of us. He shows ongoing opportunities in bricks-and-mortar businesses but also in electronic and online businesses. He offers encouragement that there are opportunities that fit you—based on your unique talents and personality.

I want to get this book in the hands of:

- The thousands of people who are fearful of the downsizing of America.
- The tens of thousands of loyal workers who have been let go by the automotive manufacturing industry.
- The mass of educators who are leaving traditional academic institutions as they diminish in providing valuable workplace application.
- The many workers who have been replaced by technology and "electronic immigrants."
- Graduating high school students—they will find extraordinary insights on success opportunities not recognized in most classrooms.

- Graduating college students—they will discover the important lesson that knowledge is merely potential power. It becomes useful only with meaningful application.
- The 71.5 million baby boomers who fear not being able to make a valuable contribution in the next season of their lives.
- Everyone who wants to turn the mundane expectations of work into a joyful and rewarding experience.

We tend to view work as a necessary evil—or even as a curse from God. *Everything I Know About Business I Learned from My Mama* will bring back the laughter and fun we should expect from the one thing that consumes the biggest chunk of our time each week.

I urge you to do something special for others and yourself—read *Everything I Know About Business I Learned from My Mama*. We can all learn from Tim's Mama.

—DAN MILLER
Author, Radio Host, Life Coach

ABOUT THE AUTHOR

As a nationally known entrepreneur, author, trainer, speaker, radio show host, business columnist, and contributing writer for Entrepreneur.com, Tim's unique perspectives on business and life are enjoyed by tens of thousands of people who read his columns or hear him speak every year.

Whether talking about business, success, motivation, life, family, kids, or dogs (he has six at last count), Tim's unique message is filled with humor and common sense: two things that are sorely lacking in the world today.

Tim has been interviewed by Fox News, the *New York Post*, ABC News, and many other media outlets on the topics of entrepreneurship, small business, and e-business.

And Tim's message is spreading fast. His online column, *"Small Business Q&A With Tim Knox,"* can be found on over 25,000 websites and that number grows every week.

Tim is the host of the weekly small business talk radio show aptly entitled "The Tim Knox Show," which is heard every Saturday from 12 noon till 2 P.M. on WVNN 770AM and 92.5FM in Huntsville, Alabama. The show is billed as "Common sense business advice with a side order of fun," and offers a unique mix of humor, entrepreneurial insight, and small business advice. The show is also carried live via the Web at TimKnoxShow.com.

Tim is also the co-host of Dan Miller's "48 Days to the Work You Love" radio show, heard every Sunday night from 6 to 9 P.M. CST on WTN-99.7FM in Nashville, Tennessee. Tim serves as the entrepreneur in residence for the show, which focuses on teaching people to get out of dead-end jobs they hate and get into careers they love.

As a serial entrepreneur, Tim is the founder and president of four successful technology companies and serves as an investor, mentor, and advisor to many companies in his hometown of Huntsville, Alabama.

As if that weren't enough to keep him busy, he is also one of the Internet's top marketers, having sold hundreds of thousands of dollars in products online in the last few years.

His newsletter, *The Tim Knox Report*, is sent to over 65,000 subscribers each week.

As a teacher, Tim is a certified FastTrac® instructor who has led numerous seminars and lectured extensively on the subjects of entrepreneurship, small business, technology, and e-business.

Prior to becoming a full-time entrepreneur, Tim spent more than 15 years as a technology executive for Boeing Aerospace and Teledyne Technologies. As a private business consultant, he led the e-business initiatives for companies such as Advance Internet, Mercedes-Benz, Time Warner, and many others.

In previous lives Tim worked as a standup comedian, a radio morning show host, an underground newspaper editor, an award-winning humor columnist, and an almost-syndicated cartoonist.

Tim lives in Huntsville, Alabama, with one wife, two kids, and six dogs. Who could ask for anything more?

For more information visit http://www.timknox.com.

ACKNOWLEDGMENTS

As any good God-fearing, biscuit-and-gravy-eating, sweet-tea-drinking, pecan-pie- (pronounced "pee-can pah") loving, dyed-in-the-wool southern boy should, I am dedicating this book first and foremost to my mother, Gertrude Knox.

My mother was the first person to tell me that I could be anything I wanted to be and do anything I wanted to do. Even though we were so poor that the white trash looked down on us (we were considered the off-white trash), she taught me that life holds no bounds for those with a hard head, a stiff spine, a quick tongue, and a true heart.

"Don't ever let anyone tell you what you can and cannot do," she would tell me. "And don't let them tell you what you can and cannot be. You show them what you can do and you will become what you're destined to be."

Her words left no doubt in my mind that the life I would lead would be the life I would build. Relying on others for your happiness and success is a fool's game. Leaving your future to fate is the lazy man's destiny. I *could* do anything that I wanted to do and *be* everything that I wanted to be. And the only person with the power to push me forward or stop me in my tracks was me.

My Mama taught me that my outcome and my income would be the direct result of my own instincts, intelligence, and initiative.

"Nobody is going to do it for you, Son. So you have to do it for yourself."

Mama supported me during the bad times and cheered for me during the good, and has never once failed to tell me that she loves me when hanging up the phone or walking me to the door.

And her meatloaf always puts a smile on my face and lights a fire in my belly, even after all these years.

So, Mama, this one's for you.

After my mother the biggest influence on my early life came from my older sister, Pat. I would not be the man I am today if not for her love, guidance, protection, and sometimes, torture. I learned to play the guitar at the age of 12 because she stood over me with a fly swatter and popped the heck out of me when I missed a note (man, talk about tough love). Some politically correct idiots would have called it child abuse. She called it motivation. Needless to say, I learned to play the guitar very quickly.

Pat was 13 when I was born and by all accounts was not initially thrilled at my arrival, but within months I was her personal rag doll and she was my biggest fan. Four decades later that relationship continues in earnest.

And then there was my amazing Aunt Rilla—my Mama's older sister, who helped raise and protect us. Rilla passed away a few years ago and it left a huge hole in my life and the lives of everyone who knew and loved her (you couldn't know her without loving her). She used to joke that her daddy traded her for a cow when she was young because he needed a cow and the other old man needed a wife. She always said the old man got the raw end of that deal because at least the cow was willing to give milk and she wasn't willing to give the old man squat.

Rilla didn't stay with the old man long. She was a free spirit who sold bootleg whiskey out her back door and refused to take orders from anyone, especially a stupid old man. For all of her 80-plus years she would rather have been kicking up her heels on the dance floor at a juke joint than tapping her toes in church, though I know in my heart that she is teaching line dancing in Heaven even as we speak.

I wouldn't be here if it weren't for her, literally. The night I was born the doctor came out of the delivery room and told Aunt Rilla that he could save me or Mama, but he couldn't save us both. Rilla threatened to kill him in his tracks if we didn't both pull through. It's amazing what medical miracles can occur when prompted by the threats of a feisty southern woman with fire in her eyes and a pistol in her purse.

I spent a lot of time with Rilla over the years and learned more from her about life than you can imagine. She is still with me to this day. I talk to her all the time and she answers me back. Maybe she'll be the subject of my next book. Boy, that would be a page turner.

I'd be remiss if I didn't mention my two brothers, Don and Sonny. My half-brother Sonny was 17 years old and in the Navy when I was born. He was one of the few examples I had growing up of what a man should be: hardworking, family oriented, dedicated, passionate, caring, funny, sober, and really, really tall. When I say I looked up to him, I mean I really looked up to him. I always thought I'd catch him height-wise when I was grown, but I missed his mark by a good six inches or so. No matter our differences in height and age, he remains one of my heroes and even after all these years I still look up to him in more ways than one.

My younger brother Don came three years after me. Mama called him a nice surprise. I called him a bad mistake. Whoever was right, it turned out that I was glad he came along. He was a funny little kid and grew into an even funnier adult. He helped make growing up in the sticks a little more interesting and a lot more entertaining. Like my older brother Sonny, Don is a good head taller than I am. They got the height, and I got the looks. I consider it a fair trade.

The other woman in my life, the woman behind the man poking him in the butt with a sharp stick, as they say, is my amazing wife, Melissa—Mel for short. She is my rock, my center, my inspiration, my best friend, my keeper, my everything. She is sometimes the biggest pain in my neck, but she also holds the keys to my heart. I think it's a fair trade . . . most days.

Like my mother, she has always had the ultimate faith in me. The difference between my wife and my mother is that my wife tells me that I can do anything I put my mind to, as long as it's all right with her.

When we met I was at a crossroads in my life. I had failed at life, both personally and professionally, and was on a definite downhill slide. I had just lost the "good job" I had held for the past 10 years and was working three menial jobs just to make ends meet and sleeping on my mother's couch because I had nowhere else to go. I owned an old junk car and a guitar and the clothes on my back and had very few prospects, but Mel saw something in me that even I didn't realize was there.

She took me in her arms and injected my battered soul with faith and love and belief and understanding. Like my mother, she believed that I had the power to dust myself off and get back in the game, and she hammered that message into my tired brain every day until I once again started believing it, too.

If not for her unbending faith in me I honestly don't know where I would be today. I certainly would not be here.

The day our eyes met was truly the day my life began anew.

And here's the funny part to this sappy little story: Despite her incredible faith and love and the fact that we've been married now for 13 (or is it 14) years, the woman has no clue what her husband does for a living.

She knows it's something to do with business and the radio and speaking and writing, but that's about as deep as it goes.

Though she will deny it, I know for a fact that she has never read a single word I've ever written, has never heard me speak to a single audience, and has never attended a single one of my training seminars.

She just knows that we live a very comfortable life and believes me when I tell her that our money does not come from the drug trade. Otherwise she is blissfully happy in her ignorance of her husband's skills.

I would have dedicated this book to her first, but she'll never read it, so why bother? The bottom line is she knows that I could never function without her. It is a fact that she reminds me of every day.

Next, I must thank God for giving me the two greatest gifts any man could ever receive: my wonderful daughters, Chelsea and Sierra. They are the shining lights in my life and my reasons for living. Each day they inspire me with a hug or a smile, or in Sierra's case, a punch in the ribs. They are Daddy's girls. They simply raise their little fingers and I start to coil around them.

As I write this Chelsea has turned 19 and is off to her freshman year at the University of Alabama. She has always believed that her daddy could leap tall buildings, and her faith in me and love for me were more than enough to see me through some very tough times. Some of the best memories of my life were times she and I spent together.

I envy her as she heads off to blaze her own trail in the world. I'm also saddened that I will no longer be the ultimate dictator to whom she reports, except when she calls home to ask for money.

My baby girl, Sierra, whom we call "Bug" because when she was little I'd always say, "You're cute as a bug," is 11 years old and is absolutely, without a doubt, the funniest person I know. She is the main source of entertainment at our house, always showing off a new dance she's choreographed or a new drawing she's sketched or telling a new joke she has made up.

"Daddy, what's yellow and lies in the grass? A dead school bus . . . Ha ha ha ha ha ha . . ."

Okay, that's really my joke, not hers. She thinks it's the dumbest joke she's ever heard, but her reaction to it every time I tell it is priceless. Feel free to use it on your own kids, with my compliments.

She is my wrestling buddy, my baby girl, and one of my "best-est" friends. I love her spirit and her passion and her innocence. She can squeeze you so tight that your spine pops and make you so mad that you want to move to a different city while she's at school. No matter, there is never a dull or depressing moment when my Bug is around.

And like her big sister, she has her daddy completely at her mercy and can usually talk me into anything, which is why I've spent many an hour scrubbing layers of makeup off my face and cutting tangled rubber bands out of my hair. Now I know why her mother refuses to play dress-up with her.

I am her plaything. She is my muse. And neither of us would have it any other way. Thanks, Bug.

There are others who have been with me down this long road and I'd be remiss if I didn't thank them for their influence and advice.

Muchas gracias (many nachos, as we say here in the south) to Vickie Sullivan of Sullivan Speaker Services, who taught me how to gather a million random thoughts and mold them into one coherent message.

Thanks to speaker and author Larry Winget, who, without the benefit of ever having met face to face, has been my greatest role model and source of education about the writing and speaking business. Larry taught me that to truly serve others you must forget *what you think they want* to hear and tell them straight-up what *you know they need to hear*.

The day I understood that simple rule my life, personally and professionally, changed for the better. Thanks, partner.

Then there's my amazing agent, John Willig, of Literary Services, Inc. I met John at a book convention in Orlando, Florida, and we just clicked. I had the good sense to seek him out between sessions and he had the good sense to listen to my elevator pitch despite my southern accent and cowboy boots. A week later he was my agent and a couple weeks after that we had a book deal. It was a good call on both our parts. John, here's to you.

And finally to Matt Holt, my editor at John Wiley & Sons, Inc., who was one of the few in New York City who truly appreciated this old redneck's down-home humor and common sense approach to business. Matt, you're all right—for a Yankee.

There have been others who have had a hand in my journey, though most will never know it. There were chance encounters and long conversations that left their mark, some positive, some negative, but all memorable.

Through it all I have tried to stay true to myself and to those who depend on me, which was sometimes hard given the path I've chosen to follow. After an investor breakfast where I was raising money for a business venture I was involved in, an angel investor sauntered over and stood looking down his nose at the cowboy boots I always wear, even when begging for angel money.

With a condescending growl he said, "I'd never invest my money in a business run by somebody who wears cowboy boots."

"What a coincidence," I said with a smile, looking down at his expensive loafers. "I'd never take money from anybody that wasn't wearing cowboy boots."

We both lied. An hour later he wrote me a five-figure check and I took it without hesitation. Were we hypocrites? Were we devoid of moral character? Can I take the Fifth?

No, we were none of those things. We were businessmen and that's the way the game is played, at least in that particular situation. I was there to raise money for a promising business and he was there to invest money and get a return on his investment. We needed each other to reach our respective goals no matter what footwear was involved. He knew it and I knew it and the other hundred or so people in the room knew it. Personalities aside, ours were puzzle pieces that interlocked perfectly despite our disdain for one another; hence the deal was done.

Business has been an adventure for me. It has been a roller coaster ride with incredible highs and unexpected lows. I have met people that I truly like and respect and I have met people that I wouldn't turn my back on for fear that they'd shove a knife into it. Unfortunately the latter group is more common than the former.

I have dealt with partners, employees, consultants, bureaucrats, lawyers, accountants, politicians, and investors. I think life would be much easier without any of them, but then again life would be much less interesting.

I have come to learn that you have to look out for yourself in business because no one else will. Nor should they. You are responsible for yourself, personally, professionally, physically, spiritually, and emotionally.

That will be a common theme throughout this book: It's all up to you. You have the power. You must choose to use it.

I have come to learn that you can be the public's golden child one day and its tarnished son the next.

I have come to learn that old men with money spend most of their time trying to figure out how to take it with them while young men with money spend most of their time trying to figure out how to waste it all away.

I have come to learn that it's not what you take with you that's important, but what you leave behind.

I hope that after I'm gone this book will remain as an inspiration to others.

At the least it should make a very nice doorstop.

Is This Book Really for You?

Whenever my dear wife is going to say something potentially insulting about someone she prefaces her comments with the words, "I don't mean this bad, but . . ."

For example, "I don't mean this bad, but if she gets any fatter she's gonna need a beeper to warn people when she's backing up."

Or, "I don't mean this bad, but that baby is so ugly they'll have to tie a pork chop around his neck just to get the dog to play with him."

"I don't mean this bad, but . . ." is her universal disclaimer.

It gives her the right to say anything she wants about anyone and still not lose points with the Big Man upstairs. Consider it sin with an out-clause.

If it's a particularly nonflattering remark she will make sure her spot in Heaven is safe by appending the statement with, "bless his heart." I call it her disclaiming double-dip.

For example, "I don't mean this bad, but that man is about as useless as a cocktail umbrella in a thunderstorm, bless his heart."

You get the idea. So, if you're standing in the bookstore reading these words right now, I don't mean this bad, but . . . this book may not be for you . . . bless your heart.

This book is written by a guy (that'd be me) who has very little tolerance for whining, lame excuses, incompetence, and sob stories; so naturally that attitude permeates my writing and outlook on life (mine and yours).

This book is the product of my experience and observations

made while building several successful businesses from scratch over the last 15 years.

This book is written in the sweat and blood of a thousand lessons learned. It offers my honest opinion and honest advice, not only on how to succeed in business, but how to achieve personal success along the way, because I believe that without personal success, business success means nothing. It's like having a Porsche in your garage, but no key in your hand. It is a hollow victory at best.

You may not share my views or respect my opinions or laugh at my jokes and I don't expect everyone to drink the Kool-Aid I'm dispensing. Only those who are thirsty for knowledge and a better life with a side order of common sense and humor will truly appreciate and benefit from what I have to say.

The rest of you . . . well, bless your hearts.

And that's okay.

Let's face it, not everyone is cut out to live a happy, meaningful life. I don't mean this bad, but . . .

Some people find great joy in spreading great pain.

Some people enjoy wallowing in their own depression like pigs in a mud hole.

Some people are happy only when they are truly miserable, or when they are making everyone around them as miserable as they are.

Some people discover that they are happy only when they do everything in their power to make themselves unhappy.

Some people torpedo themselves. Then they sit around and wonder why they always fail.

Some people will go to their graves complaining that life has done them wrong. These are the people who have things like, "I knew this was going to happen" and "Look what life did to me" chiseled on their gravestones.

Some people will die a bitter death waiting for their ship to come in and opportunity to show up at their door.

Bless their pathetic, pitiful, whining hearts.

If you are one of these people, this book is not for you.

If you're one of those people who think that everyone else on the planet is responsible for your happiness, this book is not for you.

I doubt you're one of those people because they rarely set foot in a bookstore.

"Bookstore? Is that the building down by the new Wal-Mart with all the books in it?"

Most of these goobers couldn't even tell you where the nearest bookstore is, much less give you the title of a single book therein. They do their reading in the checkout line at the food mart.

They can't tell you who wrote *Think And Grow Rich*, but they can tell you the names of all of Brad and Angelina's kids and tell you which star is sleeping with that star and how many times Elvis has been spotted in the last few years.

Now given that I believe Elvis is still alive and living somewhere in South America, we'll let that last one slide, but you get the point.

They believe in aliens and Bigfoot and *American Idol* and Jerry Springer and soap operas and reality shows and lottery tickets and hand-outs and free rides and when it's convenient, God, but they don't believe in themselves, and that's the biggest shame of all.

Next, if you're one of those people who sit on your butt with the remote control in one hand and a beer in the other while you curse fate and your fellow man because you don't live in a bigger house or drive a better car or can't afford more expensive beer, this book is not for you.

Again, since visiting a bookstore would involve actually prying your backside off the couch and taking action, I doubt this is you.

If you've ever uttered the words, "It's not my fault . . ." this book is also not for you. You're a "blame layer" and blame layers do not read books to make their lives better. They seek out books that help justify and excuse their angry existence, books that lay the blame on someone else, usually their parents or society or a past love. When they run out of physical beings to blame their problems on, they turn their anger toward a higher power and start laying the blame there.

"It's not my fault that my life stinks! God doesn't like me."

I think God must spend an awful lot of time just looking down and shaking his head, perhaps asking Himself, "What was I thinking?"

If you are constantly moaning that "life just isn't fair" this book is not for you. In fact, if you think life owes you a free ride, go ahead and put this book back on the shelf and carry your worthless butt out to the curb and sit there until the Reader's Digest Sweepstakes Prize Patrol shows up. Go on, you'll recognize them by the van and the balloons. Smile when they hand you that giant check that you think will change your life.

Say, "Cheese."

I hope you brought enough cake and punch to your pity party to share with everyone, my friend, because you're in for a long, long wait.

You may think that I'm being harsh and you may be right, but it is a harshness born out of dealing with people exactly like those I've described above.

Each example is based on real people I have encountered over the years, each of whom tried to convince me that they were willing to do everything it took to succeed in business, so long as it didn't inconvenience them or conflict with their TV viewing schedule.

We live in what I call a silver platter society, in which the majority of Americans sit and wait for things to be handed to them on a silver platter. And most often you have to put the silver platter in their lap because they are too lazy to walk across the floor to pick it up.

It's sad when these people tell me they're waiting for opportunity to knock, for their ship to come in, for their number to come up. We'll discuss later how opportunity doesn't come knocking, but even if it did these lazy goobers probably wouldn't even bother to get up to answer the door, bless their hearts.

If you are one of the people described above you don't need a book on success and you certainly have no business even thinking about becoming an entrepreneur until you make drastic changes in the way you think and the way you live your life. In your current state of mind you are doomed to failure even before you begin.

In fact, the only book you need is the telephone book. I'm sure if you flip through it long enough you'll find the name and number of someone who just might give a dang that your life is in the crapper and they may even believe you when you say it's not your fault.

As Travis Tritt would say, "Here's a quarter, call someone who cares!"

That's why my telephone number is unlisted. I live in a "no whining, no excuses" zone that prohibits such people from breathing the same air as I do.

It's a beautiful way to live. I highly recommend it.

Now that I've alienated a good portion of the population, let me tell you who should read this book and absorb it as gospel.

This book is for anyone considering a career in business, either as an owner, manager, or executive.

This book is for anyone already entrenched in a business that needs a healthy dose of common sense business advice and logical direction.

This book is not meant to be a self-help book, though I believe the principles I've used to build my businesses and under which I live my life are the same ones you can use to pursue your own dreams of success.

I believe that true business and financial success are directly related to success and happiness in your personal life. Sure, you can become wildly successful in business and still have a lousy personal life, but that means that you've only completed part of the puzzle. Until the rest of the pieces fall into place, your picture is not complete.

Your life is not balanced if the right hand is happy, but the left hand is miserable. Your success in business will one day be degraded by your lack of success in your personal life and the house of cards will come tumbling down.

I know many miserable millionaires and many happy poor people. The difference between them isn't the amount of money they have, it's the attitude with which they approach life.

You succeed personally when you and those closest to you are all happy, healthy, and living in harmony.

You are a personal success when you are loved not for the money you have and the possessions you own, but for the person you are.

You are a success when you consider others before you consider yourself.

You are a success when you get more joy out of giving than getting.

You are a success when you have earned the respect and love of those you respect and love in return.

From a personal perspective, this book is for anyone who has the backbone and determination to take responsibility for their own life.

This book is for those who know that anything worth having is worth working hard to obtain.

This book is for those who want a better life and aren't afraid of doing anything and everything necessary to build it.

This book is for those who want to live their life with purpose and intention.

This book is for drivers, not passengers.

There are a few more things you should know before you waste your money and time on this book.

One, this is not your run-of-the-mill business book. I am not going to blow smoke up your pants leg and tell you that starting and managing a business is easy, because it is not.

Even on the best of days it can be hard work, long hours, with very little reward. Being an entrepreneur doesn't mean you get to lie on the beach and drink Coronas all day. You may certainly reach that level of success, but until your business is where it can survive without your daily intervention you're going to be much too busy to even think about beaches and beer (hey, Travis, that would make a great country song title).

Two, as you've probably already figured out for yourself, I'm going to say things that tick a lot of people off. I'm not much of a coddler. I'm not going to give you my opinion and follow it up with a hug. I will not tell you what you want to hear. I will tell you what you need to hear.

I'm here to help you succeed, not to help you make excuses for your failure.

The traditional business gurus may not agree with everything I say and that's fine.

I'm not trying to help them.

I'm trying to help you.
So, is this book for you?
You are the only one who can answer that question.
Hopefully by now you know.
Bless your heart.
Now go on, pay for the dang book and let's have some fun!

ABOUT THIS BOOK

When I was asked to write this book—hang on, let me rephrase that; after I begged my agent to take me on as a client and then begged the publisher to publish this book—I spent a lot of time thinking about what I had to say and how I wanted to say it.

I understood that I possessed specific knowledge that could help other entrepreneurs and managers avoid the business mistakes I'd made and thereby improve their chances of success. The question was how to get these thoughts across to the reader in an informative, entertaining manner that would get my point across and also keep you interested and awake.

Between you, me, and the fencepost, most business books should be sold in a pharmacy in the Sleep Aid section. I don't want to sell books that put people to sleep. I want to sell books that wake them up and move them to action, not just professionally, but personally and emotionally, as well.

I don't mean this bad, my brothers and sisters, but I've spoken in front of a lot of entrepreneurs—both in the classroom and in the convention hall—and after five minutes most of them (notice I didn't use "you and me") start to look like dogs watching a ceiling fan. Their eyes are glazed over, their mouths are hanging open, and their heads are kind of nodding back and forth, seemingly in agreement, but they're not really listening.

If you suddenly yelled, "*Boo!*" half of them would have a heart attack and the other half would wet their pants. Some might even do both. While that would be fun to watch, it really would kill the point of the message. So I knew I had to write a book that would be informative, but also entertaining so as to hold the readers' attention long enough to get them hooked on my message like a snapping turtle on a trout line. Again, my hope is that you actually finish this book and put the information to good use. If you drop off after the first chapter or two you're doing yourself an injustice.

Either way, I already have your money, so who's the loser here?

It would have been very easy to just write a technical business how-to manual, but how much dang fun would that be to read? I tried to read a bunch of those books when I started my business career and I always had a hard time getting past the first chapter. If you want that sort of information, go buy one of those Dummies books, because you won't find that here.

So I decided to write a book that's part memoir, part advice tome, and part how-to manual; and often the line between them blurs, as you will discover as you read this book.

I think you can learn a lot by knowing not only where I am today, but also from whence I came and the muck and mire I had to wade through to get here. Not to mention the value of lessons learned and observations made and blunders committed and survived. By giving you insights into my past and the events that helped mold a dirt-poor kid from Alabama into a highly successful entrepreneur, I hope to open your eyes to the possibilities in your own life.

I also think that it's important that you know that when it comes to the cold, cruel world of business, you are not alone. There are millions of others out there facing the same issues and experiencing the same setbacks and victories as you. There are thousands of others who have the same questions about business that you do, thousands who are seeking similar answers and advice.

For this reason I have included questions from readers of my newspaper and online column when appropriate. I think that by reading their words and my responses, you will come to know that you are not alone and your problems are not unique. Some of the best advice I've gotten over the years came by learning from the successes and mistakes of others. Sharing these questions and answers with you lets you do the same.

The title of this book refers to the lessons on business I learned from my Mama. The truth is when you grow up in the environment I did you learn a great many lessons from a great many people.

When you start with nothing and learn as you go and build this business and that business, you also learn a great many things from a great many people.

You learn what to do and what not to do; unfortunately the latter of those lessons usually come in hindsight.

So perhaps the book should have been called, *"Everything I Know About Business I Learned from My Mama, My Sister, My Aunt, My Brother, My Old Man, My Crazy Uncle Floyd, My Mentors, My Investors, My Employees, My Accountant, My Lawyer, a Guy I Met at Radio Shack, the Dude Who Pierced My Daughter's Belly Button, My Readers, and a Whole Bunch of Other Folk."*

I was told that title wouldn't fit on the book jacket, so here we are.

One thing I've learned is this: It's not the source of knowledge that matters; it's what you do with the knowledge once you have it.

So go on, read, enjoy, learn, and act.

CHAPTER 1

How the Heck Did I Get Here?

"Tim Knox, well I'll be. I figured you'd be dead or in jail by now!"

"No, Preacher, I am still alive and roaming freely, thanks."

"Must've been all that praying I did for you back in the old days."

"Yes, sir, I'm pretty sure you are the only reason I'm still here."

I, too, am often surprised that I've made it this far in life. God knows I didn't come equipped with the best genes for success. My gene pool has been whizzed in so many times the health department sends me letters of condemnation. What success in life I have achieved has been accomplished in spite of my DNA, certainly not because of it.

With few exceptions the ancestral males of the Knox clan lacked ambition, education, and weren't especially fond of work, especially if it was hard and steady. They spent more time draining beer mugs with their pals than breaking bread with their families. Most earned little money from employment and little respect from anyone who came to know them well.

I was the first-born son and the second-born child of Claude and Gertrude Knox of Madison County, Alabama. Given their first names, I am eternally grateful that they decided to name me Tim.

This is a bullet my brother, Bubba, and my sister, Ernestine, failed to dodge. Just kidding, but wouldn't it have been hilarious if those were their real names? Hmm, probably not to them.

We were so poor the white trash looked down on us; we were considered the off-white trash. Now I get new tires for my double-wide every year, whether it needs them or not. If only the white trash could see me now.

We were so poor "fast food" meant that we couldn't catch it on foot.

When my daddy heard that the Baptist Church served fried chicken after services on Wednesday nights and Sunday mornings, we became staunch Southern Baptists. He liked to say we were led to the Lord by Colonel Sanders.

I could go on, but you get the picture.

We were not rich people.

We were also a vagabond family, moving 9 or 10 times before my 10th birthday.

Basically, when the rent came due, my old man would come home and announce that it was time to move—usually that very night.

I never realized until many years later that you could actually rent a U-Haul trailer before the sun went down. To me moving was always a nocturnal affair.

My father was a likable enough fellow who rarely held down a steady job. Of course that wasn't his fault, at least to hear him tell it. He was just about the most persecuted employee on the planet because every boss he ever had seemed to single him out for firing.

Naturally it had nothing to do with his attendance (or lack thereof) or his performance or the fact that he'd rather be drinking beer in a fishing boat than doing the work he had been hired to do.

His average time on the job, from hiring to firing, was two weeks, three at the most if a long weekend was involved.

He changed jobs as often as other men change socks. It has always been my opinion that he didn't want to work because it interfered with his drinking, which was his true talent and calling.

The old man's idea of heaven involved sitting in a fishing boat with an icy cooler containing an endless supply of Budweiser and a coffee can containing an endless supply of big, fat worms.

He'd say, "Give a man a fish and you feed him for a day. Teach a man to fish and he'll sit in the boat and drink beer with you all day long." His favorite book of the Bible was Hebrews, because he said that was the one where Jesus turned water into beer.

My old man: not much of a Bible scholar but one heck of a fisherman.

Even though he was a wash as an employee, there was a hint of entrepreneur in the old man. He was an electrician by trade and one day he decided to start his own electrical contracting business. Thoughts of legalities and licenses never entered the old man's mind, nor did the concept of discussing his intended business venture with his family. The way we found out about his new business was when he came home from the hardware store with a case of fire engine red spray paint and a pack of cardboard stencils. Oh, and the prerequisite case of beer to spur his creativity.

He drove an old blue Chevy pickup truck that no self-respecting entrepreneur would deem a suitable company vehicle. The windshield was veined with cracks because the truck had no heat, so the winter before he had tried to defrost the windshield by setting a wad of newspaper on fire and holding it to the glass. The heat from the fire cracked the frozen windshield, but did little to clear the ice. The old man called in sick that day, as I recall.

The truck was missing both side mirrors because he had knocked them off when throwing beer bottles out the windows while cruising down some dark, back country road. He taught me to drive at the age of 12 so I could chauffeur him around after he lost his license in a DUI. I guess me getting nabbed for being an under-aged driver was better than him having to do his drinking at home, where my mom would surely give him hell.

Even with its quirks, the old man was as proud of that old truck as he could be, and in his mind it had the makings of the perfect company vehicle. So he pulled the truck into the backyard, taped off the windows and the rust-pitted chrome, and proceeded to spray paint every inch of it flaming fire engine red.

He then managed to tape together a set of stencils into the words "Knox Electric" on one line and our home telephone number on the next. It never occurred to him that the phone was probably disconnected due to nonpayment of the bill. My old man didn't worry about such insignificant details. His blurred vision was much grander than that.

He let the red paint set for an hour or two before taping the stencil to the driver's side door of the truck. Using a can of white spray paint he coated the stencil and then peeled it off, then did the same on the passenger door. The white paint ran a bit, mixing with the still clammy red to form tendrils of pink, but what the heck; that was the cost of getting to market quickly. There were customers to serve, money to be made, beer to be drunk.

With a total investment of a few hours' time, a few six-packs of beer, an entire case of fire engine red and one can of white spray paint, and a couple of dollars in stencils, the first official Knox business was born.

Unfortunately, the business died a completely unnoticed death a short time later. The old man's dream of entrepreneurship vanished as quickly as it came. He quickly discovered that being in business for oneself was not as easy as he thought it would be. The phone didn't ring off the hook and the jobs did not pour in and the money did not rain down.

Plus, the paint bubbled up and started to flake off the truck within a week.

The old man learned a couple of valuable lessons from his failed entrepreneurial endeavor.

Number one: Never get drunk and spray paint a beat-up, unwashed, rusted old truck in your backyard in the middle of a blistering Alabama summer day.

Number two: Never start a business when you don't have the foggiest notion about what the heck you're doing. The old man knew nothing about business, nor did he have the desire to learn.

He just figured that other people a lot dumber than him had done it, so how hard could it be?

Accounting, legalities, advertising, networking, financing, management, leadership, customer service, and common sense were words not in his vocabulary.

To him accounting meant that he had to make excuses to my Mama for how he spent his time. Marketing was what rich people called grocery shopping. Customer service was when the man at the beer store offered him a sack to tote home his beer in.

And lesson number three was perhaps the most important one the old man learned that day: Always double-check your work.

The day he decided to paint over the faded telephone numbers on the truck doors he realized that he had gotten the telephone number wrong. Even if someone had tried to call the palatial offices of Knox Electric they'd get someone else instead, probably someone who had no idea who Knox Electric was.

I remember him standing there with a cigarette burning between his clenched lips, the spray can in one hand and a beer in the other, staring at the numbers and muttering, "Son of a . . ."

An hour later the old truck was a runny dull blue and the words "Knox Electric" never came from his lips again.

CHAPTER 2

The Day I Took a Beating in the Produce Business

My own first foray into small business was selling watermelons out of a battered red wagon that was missing the left rear wheel. The year was 1967. I was seven years old. And my old man wasn't home.

The one thing my old man was really good at was gardening. We lived in the middle of a hundred acres of cow pasture in a rented house that had no heat or air and plumbing that worked only on occasion. Surrounding the house on all sides my old man had planted huge, lush gardens.

The old man had a green thumb that ran all the way to his soul. He loved to garden and was good at it. It was one of his few sources of pride and accomplishment. He could grow prize-winning vegetables out of bedrock. Tomatoes, potatoes, corn, beans, lettuce, carrots, beets, melons; you name it; the old man could grow it. In fact, he was fond of saying, "If you can't kill it or grow it, you don't need to eat it." Needless to say, every animal on the place was nervous whenever the old man was around. Even my dog had a nervous tic. Sorry, couldn't resist.

But it was his watermelons that had caught my attention that particular fine day. I looked out over the garden and there they were, these huge green melons lying atop the dirt, calling my name.

It was at that precise moment that the first spark of entrepreneurship fired off in my brain. Fear of my father was suddenly replaced by the prospect of big profits and my first business was born.

Even then it was obvious that I was better suited for leading than following. I recruited my two best pals, brothers Jimmy and Wally something-or-other (my first employees, whose last name I can't recall), to actually do all the work while I sat under a shade tree with the wagon, propping up the wheelless corner to keep it from tilting over.

As Jimmy and Wally picked the melons from my father's garden and loaded them into the wagon, I offered keen instructions on the best way to stack our oddly shaped merchandise so that we might obtain maximum load with minimum breakage. I was a born project manager.

I took command of the wagon after it was loaded and off we went, with Jimmy and Wally taking turns holding up the crippled corner of the wagon (I quickly decided to delegate that chore).

We proceeded to knock on every door we could find up and down the county road until all the melons were sold. We repeated the process until every melon of decent size in my old man's garden was picked and sold.

Our gross revenue that day was $8.25. After paying Jimmy and Wally $1 each (big money for manual labor in those days), I pocketed a tidy $6.25 net profit and dragged my crippled wagon merrily home.

When my old man got home and discovered that his watermelon patch had been raided he forced me to turn over all the money to him (in true parental IRS fashion) and fixed my wagon, literally.

That was the day I learned an important business lesson of my own: Never enter into a business negotiation with anyone who is screaming and waving a belt at you.

I didn't know it then, but I was getting an education in business the hard way: by the seat of my pants.

I will always remember it as the day I took a beating in the produce business.

Nevertheless, I was hooked.

I was destined to be an entrepreneur.

CHAPTER 3

Maybe I Was Just Too Dumb to Know When to Quit

I'm often asked how a dirt-poor kid from the backwoods of Alabama became a successful entrepreneur who still lives in, but now owns a sizable chunk of, those same backwoods.

The answer is easy: I always knew where I was going and I always had a plan to get me there. If you had asked me 40 years ago as I stood in that barren watermelon patch where I'd be today I could have predicted the destination with pretty fair accuracy.

No, I couldn't have accurately described the route I would take to get here, but I always had the destination in mind.

It's like my Mama used to tell me, "Son, if you don't know where you're going in life, how on earth will you know when you get there?"

You don't have to be Rand McNally to know that's pretty sage advice. Would you load the family up in the car and head out on a long road trip without having any idea what your ultimate destination was?

When your kids started asking, "Are we there yet? Are we there yet? Are we there yet?" how would you know what to say other than, "Maybe . . . I don't know . . . maybe . . . I don't know."

While it's true that even if you head out with no particular destination in mind the kids will still have to stop for potty breaks every

10 miles (the human bladder has no use for a roadmap or concept of time), the journey will go much smoother when you have a final destination in mind. The same is true with business and personal success: If you don't know what success looks like and feels like and smells like and tastes like, how the heck will you know if you ever achieve it?

There is no such thing as accidental success. There is no way you can just stumble through life like a 200-pound two-year-old with no sense of purpose or direction and no talents or skills and no self-control or self-esteem and still become a raging success.

Okay, maybe if you're Paris Hilton, but not too many other people are lucky enough to be born into circumstances where all you have to do is stand there looking bored while the photographers go wild. I'm still not sure what Paris Hilton is famous for, other than being a Hilton, but the rest of America sure seems to be enamored of her. I'm sure she is the envy of every department store mannequin on the planet because lord knows she's just a notch above them in the personality and brains department, bless her heart. It's the Pinocchio syndrome: She has given hope to mannequins everywhere!

Nope, I don't believe in accidental success. However, I am a big believer in what I call intentional success. Quite simply, intentional success means that you succeed intentionally; you succeed on purpose; you succeed because you planned to, not because you were born with a silver spoon in your mouth or you won the lottery or your rich uncle died and left you a pot of gold.

I know in my heart that I am where I am today because of the roadmap I plotted out for myself many years ago. And along with that roadmap came a drive and a determination and a stubbornness born out of innocence and ignorance; I had no idea that I couldn't achieve the goals I had in mind. Other than by a few old high school girlfriends who shall remain nameless, I was never told, "No, you can't do that."

Maybe my old man summed it up best when, after watching me repeatedly try to climb an apple tree only to fall out time and time again, he told me, "Son, you'll go far in life because you're just too dumb to know when to quit."

It wasn't exactly a "life is like a box of chocolates" moment, but to me no stronger words of motivation had ever been spoken. Thanks, Dad, I appreciate the words of encouragement. My old man: the Knute Rockne of Madison, Alabama.

Climbing that apple tree was all about intention. There were big, juicy apples at the top of that tree and I fully intended to pick and eat some, no matter how many times I crashed to the ground or how hard my old man laughed each time I went "thud."

To me, succeeding accidentally or by birthright or by chance isn't really success at all. Most lottery winners are no happier than they were before they were rich, and the vast majority of them wind up broke and miserable again within a few years. One of the few differences between rich people and poor people is the quality of their problems. They all still have problems in their marriages, problems with their kids, problems with money, problems with health, and problems with attitude. The only difference is rich people have the money to buy things to momentarily make their lives seem better. They can afford pacifiers that poor people cannot.

Let's clarify the myth that money can't buy happiness. Of course money can buy happiness, you goober, at least until you figure out that having nicer stuff really isn't the key to having a nicer life. I said it earlier and I'll say it again: I know miserable rich people and incredibly happy poor people. The difference is in how they view their particular situation. You don't have to be rich to be a success in life. Success lies between your ears and in your heart, not in your bank account.

When I tell people about my poor childhood they often say, "You poor thing. You must have been miserable."

To the contrary, I have nothing but happy memories of my childhood and other than my old man's affinity for the brew, wouldn't change a thing about it even if I could.

Yes, we were poor, but my Mama and my sister made sure that we were always looked after, clothed, fed, warmed, and most of all, loved. I had a great childhood. We lived in a rickety old house that had no central heat and air and for awhile, no indoor plumbing.

The house was smack in the middle of acres and acres of pastures and woods and the nearest neighbor was miles away. We got school clothes once a year and free food from the government to supplement what we didn't grow or kill.

Once a month we'd head to the county shed to collect the food that came free from government assistance: coffee, powdered milk, mystery meat, sugar, and the best thing of all—government cheese. I loved that government cheese. It came in a block the size and shape and hardness of a brick. You could barely cut it, chew it, or melt it, but you could build one heck of a fort with it.

Would I be a better, more fulfilled, happier person today if I'd had tons of toys to play with and a new bike to ride and food that came from a store rather than a county shed? I might have thought so back then, but looking back today I wouldn't change a thing—except for maybe that indoor plumbing issue.

So you don't have to be rich to be truly happy and successful. Money is a lousy yardstick for measuring success, though I have to admit it makes the measuring a whole lot more fun.

Let's talk about where you are today. Look at your own life at this very moment—personally, emotionally, spiritually, professionally, and financially. You are where you are and you have what you have and you think what you think and you have the friends you have because of the decisions you have made up to this point.

If you live in a mobile home or a mansion, it is because of the decisions you have made.

If you drive a Yugo or a Lexus . . .

If you have a wonderful marriage or a miserable divorce . . .

If you have kids who love and respect you or kids who hate your guts . . .

If you are a joy to be around or the biggest jerk on the block . . .

Whatever the case, you are what you are because of the decisions you have made and the paths you have chosen to take since the day you were old enough for independent thought. God gave us free will to do with what we choose. Unfortunately, most people always seem to choose badly.

Your life now is the result of decisions you made years ago during brief moments you can't even recall. Such decisions may seem insignificant at the time, like choosing to turn right rather than left, choosing to stay rather than go, but they create ripples in your life that may be felt years down the road.

It's called the Butterfly Effect: one element of chaos theory that suggests the mere flapping of a butterfly's wings may create tiny changes in the atmosphere that ultimately lead to the formation (or prevention of) a tornado. In other words, tiny ripples can generate massive tidal waves; little things can lead to big results, or big consequences.

And the really wild thing is that the decisions you have made in the past and the decisions you have yet to make in the future will not only affect your life, but the lives of your loved ones and friends and people you don't even know.

Perhaps if you had left the house just a few minutes earlier that day 20 years ago you would not have been involved in that car accident that injured your back and left you in pain all these years.

Perhaps if you had taken the initiative to ask that cute girl to go to the prom you would not be so lonely today.

Perhaps if you had scanned the classifieds that day you would have seen the ad for a job that would have been perfect for you.

Perhaps if you had spent more time with your children when they were young they would visit you more today.

Perhaps if you'd been nicer to your wife she'd have been nicer to you.

Perhaps if you had been more proactive in your decision making your life would start to get better today. Some people just hate having to make a decision; they are content to just "roll with the flow" and let others tell them what to do, when to do it, and with whom to do it. Such is a life without purpose and direction, an unintentional existence.

Perhaps instead of taking charge of your life you've just let life take charge of you. It's easy to do. Life gives you lemons. Life deals you a lousy hand. Life knocks you down every time you get up.

Perhaps life has screwed you so many times and in so many ways you've just resigned yourself to take what comes. Life has made you a victim. Who are you to argue with life?

Listen, my friend, blaming life for your problems is just plain stupid. It's like blaming the cow because your ice cream melts in the summer sun because that's where you decided to eat it.

Life doesn't control you. You control life.

Destiny isn't in charge of you. You're in charge of it.

The fact is you're exactly where you are because you have gotten yourself there. You've made either bad choices or, even worse, no choices at all. If you have to be ticked at someone because your life sucks, be ticked at yourself because it is no one's fault but your own.

"But, Tim, it's not my fault that I can't get a better job. I never went to college!"

I never went to college either, Bubba, but that didn't stop me. I did drive by a college once. It looked really hard, so I kept on going.

"But, Tim, I am so deep in debt that I'll never get out! Those thieving credit card companies have got me by the short hairs and just won't turn loose!"

Those thieving credit card companies did not come to your house and twist your arm until you charged yourself neck-deep in debt. Cut up your credit cards, get on a budget, stop your whining and take control of your finances and your life. Don't make me get up and come over there . . .

"But, Tim, my wife doesn't understand me."

"But, Tim, my husband doesn't want me to be happy."

If your wife doesn't understand you maybe it's because you don't talk to her.

If your husband doesn't want you to be happy divorce the SOB and find someone who does.

Many people fail to realize that they have the power within themselves to create their own happiness and success instead of relying on others to do so. Happiness, success, harmony—all that good stuff is simply a state of mind, a state of being. It is about belief. It is a decision. You instantly become happy and successful at the moment you decide that you are happy and successful, simple as that. Too many people base their opinions of themselves on the words of others and believe they achieve success only when others say they have. It's not rocket science, but to most people it might as well be.

The power to create success, happiness, and every other emotion known to man lies between your two ears. And the old saw is true: If you can conceive it, you can achieve it. Whatever reality your brain envisions, you have the ability to create. Your brain envisions your future as a painting and hands you the brush. Admittedly, many of us paint outside the lines. And thankfully for some of us, our brains envision images that are paint-by-number; otherwise we'd be an awful mess.

I'm amazed at how most people don't realize that the keys to success are hanging on a rusty nail right inside their own pointed little head. They look outwardly for success rather than looking within. They look to the horizon for opportunity rather than in their own backyard. They look to others for happiness rather than creating happiness for themselves.

Listen, your life is yours to do with what you will. When life knocks you down, kick that sucker in the shins and get back up. When life gives you lemons, find someone that life has given vodka to and have a party. If you continually fall off the horse, shoot the nag and call a cab.

So, like the old Nike commercial, the moral to this story is: Just do it! Do something *now*. And do it intentionally. Stop living your life by accident. You will never succeed by being a victim of circumstance or life's patsy. If you had lived your life with intent from the get-go things would be very different for you today.

Living an intentional life means that you are the one in control. You are the one who plans your future and maps out your destiny. You start with an end goal in mind, and then take the steps to make it happen.

Living intentionally means that everything you do today is done to reach an end goal tomorrow or next week or in 60 years. If you decide at 20 years old that you want to retire to a tropical island at 50, then everything you do over the next 30 years is done with that tropical paradise in mind. The career you choose, the mate you marry, the money you invest, and on and on. Every step is taken intentionally, otherwise you will find yourself single and broke at age 49 and the only friends you will have are those who hang out with you in the unemployment line or sit next to you swilling booze at the beer joint on Friday night.

So let's talk about intentional success and how you can achieve it no matter where you are in life at this moment. Even if you are in a hole six feet under the bottom of the barrel, there is still hope for you. And that hope starts with the decision to climb out of that hole and create a plan to improve your life, then put that plan into action.

Figure out what you want to achieve in business and in life. Define what success means to you. Then pursue it with all the intention and purpose you can muster. That is intentional success.

In my case intentional success refers to the journey I have traveled over the last few decades and the successes I have achieved personally and professionally. Where I am in life and in business today is exactly where I have been getting to all my life. I don't think anyone who knows me doubts that for a moment. And is my journey over? Not by a long shot. There is still a lot of road left on my map. I expect I'll be traveling it right down to the day I die.

Remember, I've got a lot of miles behind me now, but I'm still too dumb to know when to quit. Ask anyone I know.

The question for you then, my friend, is: Do you know where you want to go? More importantly, will you know it when you get there?

Living intentionally is a process. It involves what I call "roadmapping." That's a topic I'll cover later in the business nuts-n-bolts section of the book. The principles of roadmapping are the same whether you are planning out your business or your life. I encourage you to read that chapter several times and put roadmapping to work for you. You and everyone in your life will be glad you did.

CHAPTER 4

A Quick Word About PMA

No business advice book would be complete without a quick word or two about the happiest little acronym on the planet: PMA or Positive Mental Attitude. I find it funny that PMA and PMS differ by just one letter, but hey, maybe I think too much.

Some well-meaning folks preach that if you just go through life grinning like the village idiot and carrying a positive attitude wherever you go, everything will be all right. Heck, I've had a positive attitude my whole life and I've had more crap heaped on me than a field of mushrooms at planting time.

The only thing I'm positive about is this: A positive attitude is a fine thing to have, but that alone is not the key to a successful life.

A positive attitude will get you only so far. Just look at most churches. They are filled with absolutely positive people who are absolutely, positively miserable. A positive attitude won't prevent bad things from happening to you (it's not a protective shield, Mr. Spock).

A positive attitude will just better prepare you to deal with the bad things when they come. And they will come. And that's a big part of succeeding personally and professionally: being prepared to deal with all the crap that life throws at you, in a positive manner, of course.

That said, a positive attitude is certainly better than a negative attitude, especially when it comes to believing in yourself and your ability to succeed in business.

Case in point: My house is overrun with dogs. At last count we had six: four of the little white puffball variety and two mutts. My wife says the puffballs are Maltese, but I call them "Swiffers" because if you strap a broom handle to them you can dust the hardwoods like a banshee; or so I'm told.

The two mutts are much more interesting dogs. We call them Shadow and Sugar, and they are the result of a union of breeds so different that most people don't believe me when I explain what you are about to read.

The mother was a 70-pound yellow Lab and the father was a 10-pound Chihuahua whose faith in his own abilities knew no bounds. Go ahead and take a moment to imagine that coupling, I'll wait.

I tend to think that a footstool and a large dose of horse tranquilizers (the doggy date rape drug) were somehow involved, but I can't be sure.

All I know is that little Chihuahua had to be the most positive-thinking pup in the state. PMA on steroids, if you will. And I'm sure that afterward he was the cockiest dog on the block. Heck, I bet the little feller even smoked a cigarette or two.

It just goes to show you that it truly is not the size of the dog in the fight that matters; it is the size of the fight in the dog. I guarantee you that little Latin lover never had a doubt that he could do the job.

Imagine how your life would be if you were that confident in your own abilities.

You, too, might be the envy of every big dog on your block.

CHAPTER 5

How to Figure Out What Success Really Means to You

We southern men have a funny way of measuring things, mainly because we believe that size matters only when you're talking about pickup trucks, televisions, and fish.

Show me a good old southern boy who has a big old pickup truck in his driveway, a big-screen TV in his den, and a big old stuffed fish (that he claims to have caught) on his wall and I'll show you a man who has discovered his yardstick for measuring success.

Success can be measured in many ways and as entrepreneurs we typically measure success by how many employees we have or how nice our office is or how much money we're making, but measuring success by the dollar may not be the best yardstick for you.

Society typically measures success with a yardstick incremented with dollar signs instead of inches. I'm sure that how many times Paris Hilton gets her face on the cover of the tabloids is one way her handlers gauge her success. Personally I'd love to see Paris's face on the side of a milk carton, but that's just my opinion.

In the good old US of A where public opinion is usually sculpted by the media and others with too much time on their hands and not enough brains in their heads, success is often measured by how much money you have, how much stuff you own, how much power you have, how big your mansion is, and so forth. And it's unfortunate that most of us use society's ideals as our own personal yardstick for success—especially we entrepreneurs, southern or otherwise.

Let me set you straight. How the outside world looks at you and how you look at yourself should be two very different things. There are many rich and powerful people who are deemed a success by society but are truly miserable when they are alone without an audience. And that's when the true measure of success should be made, not while you're standing at the judgment of others, but when you're standing in judgment of yourself.

Your own personal success should be measured in the power and number of hugs you get, the smiles you cause, and the happiness you bring. Success is best measured internally, by how you see yourself, not by how society or your mother-in-law or your boss or your employees see you.

One exercise that I take my entrepreneurial students through requires that they define exactly what success means to them in a number of areas. The point of the exercise is to make them—and you—understand that there are many kinds of success: business, financial, personal, emotional, spiritual, parental, and so forth. And they are all intertwined inside your head and your heart and your gut and your soul.

To be a complete success you can't simply excel in one area without also excelling in the others. This is an important point to keep in mind as you start your business career because the demands on you could be draining. The business may strain your relationships with your spouse and kids and may affect you personally to the point of elation or depression.

That's why it is so important in the beginning to define what business success really means to you. Will you consider yourself a success only if you build a huge business and take it public? Will you consider yourself a success if you build a small business that supports you comfortably? Will you consider yourself a success only when you can take a week off and the business keeps running without you? What effect does your idea of business success have on your personal life?

Also understand that success means different things to different people. And keep in mind that true success is not seen through the eyes of others, but through your own eyes as you look in the mirror each morning. It's how *you* see you that matters, not how your spouse, kids, relatives, in-laws, coworkers, boss, or the public at large sees you. If you truly see yourself as happy and fulfilled and successful, in the right frame of mind with the right intentions, everyone else's eyes will come to see you that way, as well.

Some folks would consider themselves a success only if they amassed great power and wealth. These are folks who buy a lottery ticket every week and live on credit cards and borrowed time. The reality is they have no clue how they would even handle such a thing as immediate wealth. Most people who win the lottery wind up miserable and broke within a few years because they discover that what they thought would be their idea of success really turned out to be just the opposite. The money just presented them with a whole new set of problems that they were not equipped to handle and their fairy tale ends in failure instead of success.

Remember, Shrek and Fiona were happy living as a broke couple in a shack in the swamp. It's when they made the trip to her rich daddy's kingdom that the trouble started.

Here is one of the most important points in this whole book: Whether in business or in life, you are a success when *you* decide you are, not when someone else pronounces you to be.

If I asked you to tell me what success means to you, what would you say? Now don't blurt out that success means having a big house or a lot of money or a hot spouse (Fabio ain't gonna show up at your door so stop wishing it) because while that may be your superficial notion of success, it may not be what success truly means to you.

I know rich and powerful folks who appear to be happy and successful on the outside, but at the end of the day their home life sucks and their kids won't talk to them and their dog wouldn't play with them if they had polish sausage strung around their neck. What these folks know down deep is what I'm telling you now: You are not truly successful until you are truly successful overall, not just in business.

When you believe that success can be gauged only by your bank account you are shooting for an ideal of success as defined by society, not by the heart. You can be successful in the eyes of others, but miserable on a personal level. Just ask Marilyn Monroe or George Reeves or Freddie Prinze or John Belushi or any of the other "successful" people who chose drugs and suicide at the pinnacle of their supposed success.

Look at the movie stars that grace the covers of all the magazines. Those people have tons of money and cool cars and big houses, but that doesn't mean they are successful, at least not in their hearts. Most would probably trade a good amount of their net worth for a little inner and outer peace.

I believe you are successful when you strive to be the best that you can be as a person. True success comes from internal peace and happiness, not from a big bank account balance.

If my kids are healthy and happy and look up to me with respect in their eyes and love in their hearts, then I consider myself to be a successful father.

If my wife looks at me with an even greater love than on the day we were married, then I consider myself to be a successful husband.

If my dogs meet me at the back door and treat me as if there is no one else on earth they'd rather see, then that confirms for me that I am successful in ways that humans cannot even gauge.

Is Bill Gates more successful than my wife, a stay-at-home mom? Bill certainly has more power and more money and more notoriety, but my wife is raising a happy family and has a husband who thinks the sun rises and sets in her eyes.

She is fulfilled and content and greets every day as if it will be the greatest day of her life.

Now you tell me, who is more successful?

If you say Bill Gates, you're an idiot, bless your heart.

Here's the exercise I give my students. List the following categories on a piece of paper: personal, emotional, spiritual, parental, spouse, family, business, professional, and if you can think of other categories, add them. The more the better.

Beside each topic write your idea of success for that topic. If your idea of success on a personal level is to be the best person you can be, with a giving heart and a caring spirit, write that down. If your idea of success on a parental level is to be a parent who loves his kids and puts their health and happiness above all others, write that down.

Next, make a list of the actions you must take to be a success in each category, along with a schedule for carrying out those actions. For example, if your idea of business success is to have your own small business that provides a comfortable lifestyle for your family by offering a quality product or service to your customers, write that down. Then list the actions you must take to achieve that idea of success. How long will it take you to achieve this level of success? How much time and money must you invest? How many hours a day will you have to work? How much traveling will you have to do? Will the business require you to be away from your family? Will you have to cut corners at home to finance the business?

After you've done this for each category take a look at what you've written. What you are now looking for are conflicts among the categories. For example, if you determined that to obtain your ideal business success you will have to be away from home for weeks at a time, that may conflict with the success plan you've created that pertains to your wife and kids.

Or if you determined that you will have to work seven days a week, that could conflict with your plan for spiritual success. The key is to identify the conflicts so you can deal with them now before they become real problems. Once you identify a conflict, create a plan of resolution. For example, if you must travel perhaps you can plan to spend more time with the family while you're at home. Or get them involved in the business so they can spend more time with you there while you're in town.

The point of the exercise is not to write your life in stone, but to help you understand that every area of your life is affected by every other area and as you start your business career you would be wise to keep that in the forefront of your mind.

Your business life will spill over into your personal life and your personal life will spill over into your relationships and your relationships will spill over into your professional commitments and on and on and on.

Figure out what success means to you on all levels—not just in business—and you'll be amazed at how quickly you attain it.

CHAPTER 6

When Business Stops Being Fun, Get Out of Business

One of the very few times I attempted to bond with my old man I almost ended up electrocuted to death and he ended up on the ground rolling around and laughing like a deranged pig wallowing in a mud hole.

I was in my early teens and he was working on some old car in the backyard. Looking back now I realize it was a stupid thing to ask, but I said, "Anything I can do to help?"

To which he replied, "Sure, Son, hold this plug wire while I rev up the motor."

Now I have to admit that I did not then (and still don't today) know a spark plug from a fire plug, but ignorance alone was never enough to stop me from diving in with both feet. So there I stood in all my youthful innocence and naïveté, holding the end of a frayed plug wire to the best of my abilities.

My father—or at least the man who claimed to be my father— climbed inside the car and slammed his foot on the gas, revving the engine and sending one hell of a spark through that wire.

Needless to say that spark raced through the wire and into my hand and up my arm and across my chest and though my body and down my legs and back up the other side until it landed in a tender area with ties directly to my soul. I let go of that wire and fell to the ground screaming bloody murder, knowing full well that my chances of ever having children or a deep voice had just been greatly diminished.

My old man (he ceased being "father" at that point) came around the car and fell to the ground beside me laughing like a cracked-out hyena. He took a long look at his poor, injured son who was screaming and writhing on the ground beside him and said, "For Pete's sake, Son, it didn't kill you. That was funny. You really need to lighten up."

I'd like to tell you that those heartfelt words of comfort made me feel better about my injured body and warped DNA, but that would be a lie. They did stop my crying simply because it's hard to weep when you're plotting horrific revenge.

A few days later I stuck a chicken snake under the seat of the old man's truck, which he discovered while traveling at a fairly high rate of speed, but that's another story.

I did learn one thing from that episode and that is this: You have to learn to laugh, at life and at yourself. We humans take ourselves way too seriously most of the time. We laugh at TV shows and funny movies and monkeys at the zoo and the guy at work who wears his pants up under his armpits and black socks with sandals, but we'd be doing ourselves a world of good if we could learn to laugh more at ourselves.

Laughter, especially the self-deprecating kind, is an important part of success. When you can laugh at yourself the whole world seems a little lighter. It's hard to be angry and depressed when you're laughing.

I hear people complaining all the time that their business is killing them, that they hate their customers, that they're not having any fun. Heck, I've said it myself on occasion and I'm sure you have, too. We're only human, after all; whining is what we do best.

I won't pretend that every moment of my career has been a laugh riot because it hasn't. Business is tough and sometimes there is nothing funny about it. Many days are overwhelming, filled with disappointment and regret. There are times when you'd rather kill your employees and string up your customers than look at them. There are days when you just want to fall on the ground and cry like a kid who's just been electrocuted by a father with a demented sense of humor and a hard lesson to teach.

And the lesson was, for those of you who missed it: Learn to lighten up. Learn to laugh. Learn to enjoy your business. Learn to plow your way through the bad and revel in the good.

Business should be fun. That's why we do it. When it stops being fun that's when I start looking around for something else to do.

As Dudley Moore said in the classic movie, *Arthur*, "Isn't fun the best thing to have?"

And if you happen to be the guy with the pants up to your armpits and the black socks and sandals, spend some time in front of a mirror. The laughter will do you good.

CHAPTER 7

A Tale of Lightbulbs and Red Tape

People go into business for a variety of reasons: to make a lot of money, to be their own boss, to build an inheritance for their kids, to be in control of their own destiny, because they're idiots and don't know any better—bless their hearts, and on and on.

My main motivating factor for finally striking out on my own (other than a burning desire in my gut that for years I thought was acid reflux) was that I just got sick to death of swimming in corporate red tape and putting up with upper managers that I felt didn't have the common sense to come in out of the rain.

And the corporate BS was overwhelming for a guy like me who is best suited working for himself. A secret government study revealed that there is more methane gas emitted by big corporations than from all the cattle ranches and dairy farms in the country combined. Naturally big business put the kibosh on the release of that study so the only people who know about it are the guy who compiled the numbers and me.

Well, and now you.

And the guy who did the survey disappeared mysteriously last year.

Let me tell you a true story about corporate BS and its partner in crime, Mr. Red Tape. If you've spent any time serving in the big house of corporate America, you'll relate to this story and undoubtedly have one of your own.

I spent years working for a very large defense contractor. I can't tell you the name of the company because their corporate attorneys would probably come after me for revealing their top secret company policies, but I can tell you it rhymed with "Bow and Arrow Space" and they sell a lot of airplanes.

One day a 60-watt lightbulb in a lamp in my office blew. I assumed that replacing this lightbulb would be a very simple matter of calling down to the facilities department and asking them for a lightbulb. Now therein lies the first lesson on corporate red tape: At a big company there is a department for everything. I even think there is a department that just sets up other departments.

"What are you in charge of?"

"I run the Department Department. I'm the Department Department Manager"

Lesson number two: Even though replacing a lightbulb should be a simple matter of unscrew the old and screw in the new, in a large corporation there is no such thing as a simple matter. There is one whole department dedicated to complicating things. It's called the Complications Department and that's where they send you after you've flunked out of all the other departments.

So I pick up the phone and call down to the facilities department and I say, "Yes, a lightbulb in my office lamp blew. Can I come down and get a new bulb, please?"

You'd have thought that I had asked to come down and kiss his sister on the mouth because the guy on the other end yelled back in my ear:

"What? Come down and get a new bulb? Are you nuts? No, you can't come down and get a new bulb. That's not how we do things here. Who the heck do you think you are?"

"Well, I think I'm a guy who's sitting here in the dark."

"What are you, some kind of comedian?"

"Well, yes," I said. "But only on weekends."

Look, I'm not the sharpest crayon in the box, but I knew this guy wasn't going to laugh at anything I had to say. So I tried to get back on track by asking, "Okay, let's start over. What do I have to do to get this lightbulb replaced?"

"Well, you have to come down here to my office in Building 10 and fill out a facilities request for the lightbulb and then someone from facilities will come up with the lightbulb and install it for you."

"So I have to come down to your office in a totally different building and fill out a form requesting a new lightbulb."

"That's right."

"Then you will send someone over to my office in this building with a lightbulb and they will install it for me."

"That's right."

"And I assume by 'installing it' you mean they'll unscrew the old bulb and screw in the new one."

"That's right. And they'll bring a form that you have to sign stating that the lightbulb has been installed."

"And that whole process makes sense to you?" I asked.

He gave a little snort and said, "That's the procedure, bud. Sense has nothing to do with it."

Well, I couldn't argue with that. Still, this whole process seemed more than a little bit convoluted to me. So I said, "Now here's a thought, when I come down there to fill out the form requesting that you replace the lightbulb in my office, why don't you just hand me the lightbulb and I will install it myself. I mean, I've had no formal training in installing a lightbulb, but I'm pretty sure I could handle it myself."

Boy, was that the wrong thing to say. Bubba Jim on the other end of the phone got so irate that I thought he was going to bust a blood vessel.

"What? Didn't you listen to me before? That's not how things are done. You can't install the lightbulb yourself. You don't work for facilities. What are you trying to do, put one of my guys out of work?"

Now the last thing I wanted to do was to put anybody out of work, especially a trained lightbulb installer. I just wanted a little light in my office!

"Look, I'm sorry, the darkness is just getting to me, I guess," I said.

"Okay, so I come down and fill out the form and you send someone up to replace—I mean, install the lightbulb and we're good to go."

"That's right."

"And how quickly would you be able to get someone up here with that lightbulb once I've filled out all the appropriate forms?"

"Lemme see . . ."

I hear him muttering to himself. I could make out the words, "Monday . . . no, Tuesday . . . no . . ."

He comes back on the phone and says, "I can have someone up there Friday between noon and 5 P.M."

"Friday between noon and 5 P.M.?" I repeated. Who the heck did this guy work for, the cable company? "That's five days from now."

"That's right."

"But I have to come down there today and fill out the request form?"

"That's right. If you want the lightbulb by Friday you need to fill out the request today. We schedule out five days in advance."

"So I have to sit in the dark for five days?"

"Hey pal, I'm squeezing you in on Friday," he said.

"Right, and I appreciate that," I said. "Let me ask you something totally off the record, just between you and me. Let's say hypothetically that I bring in a lightbulb from home and install it myself just to get me out of the dark until Friday. Would that be okay with you?"

He started yelling in my ear again. "What? Are you crazy?"

"No, dude, I'm not crazy, I'm just afraid of the dark!"

"Listen, fella . . ."

He actually called me *fella*. I suddenly felt like a Golden Retriever.

"If you attempt to bring a foreign lightbulb onto company property, then attempt to install the lightbulb in a company-owned lamp, you are violating about a dozen union rules and company policies. You will be guilty of bringing an unauthorized lightbulb onto company property and tampering with company property. You know what would happen if you did that?"

"Um, I'd have light?"

"No, you'd be fired!" he yelled.

"You're telling me that if I bring a lightbulb from home and screw it into this lamp, I could be fired?"

"That's right!"

"That is a fire-able offense?"

"You bet your badge it is."

"But if I come down to your office and fill out a form someone from your department will be here with a lightbulb in five days?"

"That's right."

"And that policy makes sense to you?"

"Sure it does," he said. "That's the way it's always been done."

Ah, *that's the way it's always been done*, the most-used corporate excuse on the planet.

So I hung up the phone and was about to feel my way across my darkened office toward the door so I could walk down two flights of stairs and across a huge parking lot to the building that housed the facilities department and fill out this stupid form, when the phone rang.

It was the manager in charge of the Security Department, who informed me that the facilities manager had just reported that I should be considered a security risk because I had asked about bringing a foreign lightbulb onto company grounds.

"A foreign lightbulb?" I said. "Oh, no, sir, this would be an American lightbulb, I'm sure."

He was not amused. He told me to report to his office so he could formally educate me on the rules and regulations governing foreign lightbulbs and the ramifications of abusing the company lightbulb policy.

I said fine, where is your office.

He said in Building 10, right next to the facilities department.

Great, I thought, I can kill two very stupid birds with one stone.

After being read the riot policy by the security manager, I walked across the hall to the facilities department and filled out the lightbulb replacement request form.

And what do you think I saw on the shelves behind the counter? Lightbulbs: boxes and boxes of beautiful lightbulbs. Oh so near, and yet so far.

CHAPTER 8

Maybe I Just Think Too Much

I haven't always been the diehard entrepreneur you have before you today. To the contrary, I was raised to believe that once you finished your schooling you found a "good job" and did your best to hold on to that good job until the day you died.

"Good jobs are hard to come by," I remember hearing from the older men in my family, most of whom had never found that occupational Holy Grail themselves, which was why they spoke of it with such awe. "You find a good job you better hold on to it for dear life."

And so I did. After several career sidesteps, which included time as a radio announcer, an insurance salesman, a pest control technician, and a night club DJ, I landed a job as a technical illustrator with a large defense contractor. It was good pay, good benefits, and a good future. I felt a little like Indiana Jones on career day: I had found the good-job Holy Grail and to take it away from me you would have to pry it from my cold, dead hands.

And so for many years I became the model employee, the proverbial company man. I gave the company 150 percent and was employee of the month more than once. I willingly came in early and often stayed late. I worked weekends and holidays and any other time the job called.

I was dedicated. I was a hard worker. I loved my good job.

But—there's always a "but"—I was also the squeaky wheel in the organization. I was always coming up with ideas on how to make things run smoother, how to cut hours and increase productivity; how to manage work flow better, how to do this and that better, faster, or cheaper.

I didn't realize it at the time, but I was an "intrapreneur;" an employee with an entrepreneurial slant. Intrapreneurs think like entrepreneurs, only within the confines of the company environment. And intrapreneurs can be an asset or a hindrance to a company, as I was soon to find out.

Most of the managers I reported to over the years understood my need to come into their offices and spew ideas like water from a deranged sprinkler. Some of my ideas were implemented, some were not. That really didn't matter to me. The point was that my ideas were listened to and acknowledged, but never ignored.

Then one day a new manager took over the division and he wasn't quite as willing to listen to this crazy guy with his innovative ideas. He made it very clear from the start that he wasn't interested in hearing what I had to say. He was an old company man who did everything by the time clock and the job description. The last thing he needed was an "idea guy" on his staff. And the last thing I needed was some old fart telling me that my input and ideas were unwelcome. Our relationship was always cordial, but needless to say we had very different opinions on how things should work.

Despite his resistance, I'd come into his office at least once a week with a new idea and he'd lean back in his chair, close his eyes and nod. At the time I thought he was just basking in my brilliance. I now believe he was just nodding off.

One day, after sitting silently through another of my pitches he let out a long breath and said, "Knox, you think too much."

Now this was a new one on me. I had been accused of not thinking enough and I had been accused of not thinking at all. But never had I been accused of thinking too much.

"Look," he said, "for the last time, just go back to your office and do your job and forget all these ideas you're always coming up with.

The company is running fine without your input. Do us both a favor and stop thinking so much."

"Okay," I muttered. Honestly, I didn't know what else to say. I was, after all, just trying to help, and just following my nature. Telling me not to think was like telling me not to breathe. It was not something I could do.

So I tucked my tail between my legs and walked slowly back to my office. And with each step I began to think. I thought about all the years I had invested with the company. I thought about the fact that my plan had always been to stay with the company until I retired or died. I thought that maybe everything I had thought over the years was suddenly all wrong.

So I began a journey that day on a new train of thought. I started thinking that perhaps I really wasn't suited for the big company career trek, after all.

I started thinking that I would never really be happy unless I was working for myself.

And finally I started thinking about planning my exit.

Within six months the little home business that I started as a result of that meeting was bringing in enough money to match my salary. So I thought I would take the leap.

I walked into my manager's office and said, "I think it would be best if I left the company."

I can still recall the stunned look on his face as he said, "Huh?"

"I'm going into business for myself," I said. "Consider this my two weeks' notice."

He just tossed his pen to the desk and shook his head. "Well, Knox, I guess you gotta do what you gotta do, but personally I think you're nuts."

I just smiled and said, "Sir, perhaps you think too much."

I have never looked back.

CHAPTER 9

Serial Entrepreneur Doesn't Mean You Manufacture Breakfast Food

Many years later I discovered that there are two kinds of entrepreneurs: those who start one business at a time and give it 100 percent of their time and attention, and those who start multiple businesses and give each of them 100 percent of their time. I know that adds up to more than 100 percent, but that's why I'm an entrepreneur and not a mathematician.

The latter is known as a Serial Entrepreneur. A Serial Entrepreneur is one who is never satisfied with just one business. Oh no, that would be too easy. A Serial Entrepreneur is one who is always looking for his next business, even when he's neck deep in his current business.

You might think that Serial Entrepreneurs lack focus. That's not true. Serial Entrepreneurs have tons of focus. Like manure on a rose garden, we just spread it around among a dozen different ventures and expect them all to grow and thrive.

I'm a confessed Serial Entrepreneur, and no, that doesn't mean I peddle breakfast food for a living. It means that I simultaneously run multiple businesses. Sometimes I run them well and sometimes

I run them in the ground. The running of multiple businesses isn't what cranks my tractor. The rush is in the starting, not in the running. Serial entrepreneurship is not for everyone. Running multiple businesses is a lot like dating multiple women who demand all your time and all your money and all your attention, and threaten to give you a massive coronary or at least bankrupt you if they don't get it.

Here are a few ways to tell if you're a Serial Entrepreneur:

You find a stack of business cards in your desk that have your name listed as the president of at least 10 different companies, some of which you don't even remember starting.

You've signed more office leases than Donald Trump.

You've mortgaged your house so many times to finance various business ventures that you will eventually have it paid off . . . in the year 3025.

You lie awake at night thinking up cool domain names just so you can build a business around them.

The lady behind the counter at the business license department has pictures of *your* kids on her desk.

When someone asks you what you do for a living you say, "I work for myself," and you actually believe it.

You've muddled through so many business ventures that you learned a few things along the way and now people think you're some kind of business expert and the local paper gives you your own business advice column and some wacky publisher gives you a book contract.

Man, is this a great country or what?

CHAPTER 10

Burning Out Like an Old Muffler

At one point in my business career I started burning out like the muffler on my old man's pickup truck. I was running multiple businesses, writing a weekly newspaper column, writing a monthly column for Entrepreneur.com, consulting with clients, teaching entrepreneurship classes, dealing with one wife, two kids, six dogs, and on and on and on.

The straw that broke the camel's back was when I woke up in a Kansas City hotel and for a moment, couldn't remember why I was there. I was pretty sure I was there on business rather than pleasure (I don't mean this bad, but it was the Kansas side, after all, bless your heart), but that was about it.

It was at that moment that I discovered that I had done what many entrepreneurs before me had done and many entrepreneurs since: I had stretched myself thinner than a fat lady's wonder bra and I just snapped—in Kansas City in the middle of winter, of all places.

Why is it that we never snap in a place like Maui?

The sheer demands on my time and limited brain power had finally caught up with me. I had overloaded my circuits and as I drank my second cup of lousy hotel coffee and partook of the equally lousy free continental breakfast, I realized that if I didn't make changes fast, I would soon melt down, mentally and physically.

The mental breakdown worried me the most because that was a tightrope I had walked since birth. Every monkey in my family tree was mentally off-balance in some way. Some of us just managed to keep it hidden better than others.

The only certifiably crazy Knox that I had ever known was my great-uncle Luther, who would walk back and forth in front of a relative's house (or a house he believed to be inhabited by relatives) with a large bag of rocks on his shoulder until they invited him in for a meal. He'd come in without saying a word, eat his fill, pick up his bag of rocks, and be on his way again.

And if you didn't invite him in quickly enough he'd start throwing rocks at your house until you did.

On really hot days he'd forgo the formality of the back-and-forth pacing and just start throwing rocks.

You had a choice of his company for a meal or a few broken windows in your house. Since all of the Knoxes were dirt poor and replacing a window cost a heck of a lot more than a pan of biscuits and a bowl of gravy, uncle Luther usually ate very well.

So I finished my business in Kansas City, flew home, and decided to go on hiatus. I was not taking a sabbatical. I was not going on vacation. I was not taking a break. I was not going to decompress.

I was going on hiatus.

Why on hiatus, you ask?

Mainly because I just liked telling people, "Hey, guess what? I'm on hiatus."

It made me sound much more important than I really was.

Unfortunately, most folks in Alabama don't know what the word "hiatus" means, so I just got a lot of stupid stares.

My mother, for example, thought that I had quit working because I was inflicted with a life-threatening hernia.

She worried herself sick over it until I told her that I was just taking some time off to recharge my batteries. Then she thought I was having problems with my car and just started worrying about that.

While on hiatus, I decided to analyze the path that had brought me to the brink of becoming a rock thrower. I sat down with a legal pad and pen and took inventory of everything that I was involved in and started setting priorities. Before that moment I had no set priorities. Everything was job one. Everything was important. Everything screamed for my attention.

I was like an old hound dog that had lost its sense of smell. Many days I got nothing done because I couldn't figure out which rabbit to chase first.

I knew that I had to focus more on fewer projects and withdraw totally from projects that didn't depend on my involvement. I had to pursue things that made personal and economic sense and walk away from things that didn't.

I scrapped plans to start more businesses and formulated plans to improve the businesses I had. I delegated work to my employees and gave more responsibility to my top people. I stopped taking every phone call and personally answering every e-mail. I learned the value of the word "No."

My hiatus lasted less than a week, mainly because my loafing around the house all day got on my wife's nerves so she suggested it would be best for her sanity, my personal safety, and our marriage if I went back to work.

So back to work I went, only this time I did so with the understanding that I'd have to make a few changes to keep from burning out again.

Little by little, I regained control of my business and personal life. For the first time in years I was working less than 16 hours a day and sleeping more than 3 hours a night.

I reconnected with my wife and my kids and my dogs.

I started taking my mother to lunch every week.

I learned that it's not how many businesses you own, it's how well you run those you already have.

And until you can control space and time, there have to be limits on how much you can do. No matter how hard you try it is impossible to add a 25th hour to the day. Trust me; I've tried.

Was this process hard for me? You bet. I'm a card-carrying serial entrepreneur and expecting me to not think about business is like expecting a teenage boy not to think about sex. I'm an entrepreneur by nature. Starting businesses is what I do. The key, I have now learned, is that I must do it all in moderation.

Business has turned into a 12-step program for me. I know that I could fall off the wagon tomorrow if a tasty venture came along, but for now, so far so good.

At least my mother doesn't have to worry about her son's nasty hiatus anymore.

And yes, Mama, my car is fine.

CHAPTER 11

Are You Just Waiting for the Right Opportunity to Come Along?

My Mama used to say, "Son, there are two kinds of people in this world: those who do and those who don't."

She forgot to mention those that pretend to do, but really don't do much of anything.

"Doers" are those folks who take charge and get it done. Doers don't wait for things to come along. Doers get up every morning and leave the cave early and go out into the cold, cruel world and kill something and drag it home.

The "Don'ts" of this world approach life differently. They're laidback and lazy, content to drift through life without much purpose. They get up whenever they feel like it and sit on a rock out front of the cave and wait for a Doer to come by in hopes that they will share their catch with them.

Don'ts are content to just sit and watch the world go by.

Doers are content only when they have the world by the horns.

Are you a Doer or a Don't? Or maybe you're a "Can't" or a "Won't"? While this all may sound very much like *The Cat in the Hat*, when it comes to business, Doers succeed, others don't; it's as simple as that.

Don'ts are famous for saying things like, "I'm just weighing my options. I'm looking at a variety of possibilities. I'm just waiting for the right opportunity to come along." People, please, don't make me come over there and beat you to death.

I hate the Don'ts of this world, especially when they proclaim themselves to be entrepreneurs like me. They come up to me all the time and profess their admiration and tell me how much alike we are. I'm like a Don't magnet for some reason. I personally think it's God testing my tolerance for idiots so He'll know where to put me in the afterlife. Please, God, not customer service . . .

They come up to me all the time, gushing, "Tim, I'm an entrepreneur, too, just like you! Ain't that great? I'm just waiting for the right opportunity to come along, then I'll dive right in! We should start a club or something! Hey, we should start a business!"

Bubba, if I had a club you'd be a dead Don't.

If I hear just one more of these armchair entrepreneurs say, "I'm just waiting for the right opportunity to come along," I think I will plant my cowboy boot so far up their backside that they can taste boot polish.

Opportunity is not delivered like pizza.

You don't hear a knock on your door and open it to find some pimply-faced teenager in a crooked baseball cap and baggy pants holding a piping hot box of opportunity.

Opportunity does not come along.

Opportunity does not knock.

Opportunity doesn't even know where you live.

Opportunity doesn't know your name, your phone number, or your personal situation.

Opportunity does not appreciate your talents, your skills, or anything else about you.

Opportunity does not care that you are a great person who just needs a chance.

Doers do not wait for opportunity to come along; they seek it out. They get up off the couch or get out of their cubicles, go out the door, and run up and down every street in town knocking on every door they come to. Sometimes opportunity answers the door, sometimes not, but real entrepreneurs keep knocking.

Doers know that you can knock on a thousand doors and never find opportunity waiting on the other side. They also know that opportunity might be waiting just at the next stop, so they keep finding doors and they keep knocking.

When people ask where I went to business school I give them the standard reply: The School of Hard Knocks. But I don't mean that life has beaten me up on my way to where I am today. I mean that I went up to a lot of doors and knocked as hard as I could and every now and then, opportunity answered. Am I a success because I sought out opportunity rather than waiting for it to come to me?

You bet, and I have the bruised knuckles to prove it.

CHAPTER 12

Be a Serious Entrepreneur—The World Has Enough Contractors

Earlier this year I was convinced by my loving wife and adoring kids that if I truly loved them I would have a swimming pool installed in our backyard.

Now, I personally believe that if God had meant for humans to spend time in the water He would have given us gills instead of ears and fins instead of fingers and flippers instead of toes, but who am I to argue with the wishes of the water-lusting women in my life? Hence the large cement pond that now takes up most of my backyard.

The experience did introduce me to an interesting class of entrepreneurs collectively called "contractors." I don't mean to generalize, but the contractors I've been dealing with are a stereotypical bunch of good old boys who drive really big pickup trucks and wear worn work boots and dirty jeans and torn t-shirts and sport ratty whiskers and go by names like Buddy, Bubba, Junior, Earl, and of course Tiny, who was the largest guy on the crew.

Side note: Naming a fat guy Tiny is like naming a three-legged dog Lucky or a one-armed man Lefty or a bald guy Harry. Sure, it's funny at first, but then the joke, like the seat of Tiny's pants and the fuzz on Harry's head, wears thin.

So I gave my wife the okay for the pool (like she needed my approval) and the contractors started coming out of the woodwork.

There was the pool contractor, the concrete contractor, the landscaping contractor, the fencing contractor, the hole digging contractor, the dirt-from-the-hole removal contractor, the pest control contractor, the electrical contractor, the plumbing contractor, and contractors whose specialty I've since forgotten.

Then the fun began as the contractors began to disrupt our lives. And the one question that kept going through my mind throughout the entire ordeal was this: How in the name of Grandpa Jones do these guys manage to stay in business since they apparently don't give much thought to the usual rules of business, choosing to ignore little things like sticking to their estimates and scheduling and keeping appointments and being where they said they would be when they said they would be there and keeping their employees in line and securing the required licenses and ensuring quality of work and respecting their customer's property, and on and on.

Now I mean no disrespect to the contracting industry as a whole. I'm sure there are many upstanding, honest, hard-working contractors in this world who take great pride in their work and do business by the book and give more than a cup full of tobacco spit about their customer's wishes and satisfaction. Then there was the crew that took up residence in my backyard for the better part of the summer.

From them I learned a few valuable lessons about the contracting business that I'd like to share with you now. If you've ever dealt with a contractor of any kind I'm sure these lessons will ring familiar to you.

When a contractor says, "Yes, sir, we'll be out first thing in the morning," he really means, "Well, sir, if you're lucky we'll be out here at some point over the next 6 to 12 months and we won't bother calling to let you know that we're not coming or to reschedule. We'll just show up and act like everything is all right and work a few hours before we disappear on you again."

When a contractor says, "Yes, sir, that's probably gonna be about a thousand dollars," he really means, "Well, sir, I have no idea how much that's gonna cost, but I can guarantee you it's gonna be way more than you expect to pay. We'll start at a thousand dollars and work our way up, how's that?"

When a contractor says, "Yes, sir, we can get her done in about a week," that really means, "Well, sir, I can't predict the future. The thing will be done when it's done, period."

When a contractor says, "Of course I guarantee my work," he neglects to add, "If you can find me."

Contractors are like renegade entrepreneurs: They want to be in business for themselves, but on their terms. If you and I approached business with the same lackadaisical attitude we wouldn't be in business very long.

Here are the lessons learned that you should put to work in your business.

When you offer a bid on a job, honor its terms.

When you promise a price, don't go over it.

When you set an appointment with a customer, keep it.

When you commit to a schedule, stick to it.

When you get the job, finish it.

When something goes wrong, fix it.

Now how hard is that?

So, now that I've ticked off every contractor within reading distance, let me say this: According to my deeply tanned wife and shriveled-up kids, the end result was worth the hassle.

Even I have to admit, the pool turned out great.

My wife is happy.

The kids are happy.

The contractors are happy.

And I'm told that I should be happy because my family is happy and that's what counts.

I do feel better now.

Venting to you always makes me happy.

CHAPTER 13

There Is No Such Thing as a Perfect Entrepreneur

I was asked the other day what personality traits I thought were important to entrepreneurial success. I gave the standard reply about passion and perseverance and hard work and *blah, blah, blah, blah*.

I really didn't mean to shortchange the person asking the question, it's just that I have been asked that question so many times that the answer automatically drones from my lips without the involvement of my brain, kind of like when my wife asks, "Does this make me look fat?" and without looking up from the television I automatically respond, "No, dear, it makes you look thin; incredibly thin."

Since I know at some point in the future someone will ask me to expand on my fortune-cookie answer, I decided to come up with a more comprehensive profile of the perfect entrepreneur. This will help me avoid looking like a total goober who just makes stuff up and passes it off as wisdom and hopes nobody ever notices—not that I've ever done that; really, I never have.

First understand that like the perfect man, the perfect plan, and the perfect crime, there really is no such thing as the "perfect" entrepreneur, so the following list of the most desired entrepreneurial traits should be taken with the same grain of salt as the list my wife compiled before we were married regarding the perfect husband.

She settled for 2 out of 10 and it's worked out okay so far for her, so don't be too devastated if you come in on the short end of the stick, too.

So without further ado, or adoo, as we spell it here in the South, I present you with the official Top 10 List of personality traits most commonly found in successful entrepreneurs.

Consider it a test and give yourself 1 point for each "Yes" answer and a big fat *zero* for each "No."

1. *Can you delegate without micromanaging?* Running a business requires the performance of dozens of simultaneous tasks and it's foolish to try to handle them all yourself, even though that may be the case until you can afford to hire help. You must surround yourself with partners and employees whom you can trust to perform these tasks as you would yourself. If you can't dish out responsibility without worrying over the result, add a zero to your score.

2. *Are you self-motivated and disciplined?* If you do not have the wherewithal to bounce out of bed each day without your spouse drenching you with cold water, chances are you don't have the self-motivation and discipline required to be an entrepreneur.

   Business demands that you take action based solely on your own volition. You have to motivate yourself to pick up the phone and make sales calls. You have to motivate yourself to get in the car and visit customers. You have to do a hundred things every day that will not get done unless you make yourself do them.

3. *Are you willing to work hard for as long as it takes?* Starting a business is easy, right? *Wrong!* If you think working for someone else is hard work, try starting your own business. You will be required to give every ounce of blood, sweat, and tears you can muster. You will have to work long hours and be on call 24/7, at least in the beginning. If the mere thought of hard work makes you tired, congratulations, here's your zero.

4. *Are your personal relationships strong enough to withstand starting a business?* The first question I ask anyone who tells me they want to start a business is: "What does your significant other think?"

When you start a business you may have to spend more time away from the family than you like. The business may also put a strain on you financially. And what puts a strain on you puts a strain on your family, so don't think you're taking on the world alone.

You will have enough obstacles in your way without having to worry if you have the support of your family and those closest to you. If your family isn't supportive, give yourself a goose egg.

5. *Are you willing to be your best salesperson?* This is a triple-zero question since every business requires revenue to survive no matter how deep its pockets and in the beginning it will be up to you to get the dollars flowing in. And dollars come from selling: selling yourself and selling your products. Yes, I said "selling yourself," that is, convincing the customer that they can trust you and that doing business with you is a wise thing.

Even though dealing with customers is one of the most basic fundamentals of business, selling—both face-to-face and over the telephone—presents a huge brick wall for many entrepreneurs. I've known entrepreneurs who would literally break out into nervous hives at the mere thought of trying to sell something to someone. They would rather move in with the in-laws than ask someone for the sale. That's one of the things about doing business online that appeals to most entrepreneurs: You rarely have personal interaction with customers. Everything is done by e-mail. The in-person aspect goes away. Sending an e-mail is not nearly as nerve-racking as talking in person or on the phone. We'll go deeper into this later in the section on Internet business.

So, how about you? Do you cringe at the thought of going for the close? Asking for the sale? How about cold-calling, that is, walking into a business without notice and asking to speak to the owner. Is that something you think you could do?

Can you pick up the phone, call a prospect, and ask for an appointment without breaking into a cold sweat? If you are not comfortable selling and can't afford to hire someone to do it for you, you will have a very hard time making it in business. Zero, zero, zero.

6. *Can you pick yourself up and get back in the game when business knocks you down?* My Mama always said, "If it was easy, everybody would do it." In business that statement is especially true. Starting a business is hard work and the odds for failure are stacked squarely against you in the first few years. If you want to ride herd on your own business, you must be willing to fall off your horse a few times without giving up. If you can't dust off your pants and ignore the bruises and climb back on, you've just roped yourself a fat zero.

7. *Can you handle rejection?* How thick is your skin? If your feelings are easily hurt, keep your day job because business is not for you.

Many days in business, rejection waits around every corner and you must be able to handle rejection without letting it beat you down.

You will experience rejection from customers, business partners, bankers, and investors, just to name a few.

If you can't take "no" for an answer without getting your feelings hurt, don't quit your day job.

8. *Do you interact well with others?* Being an entrepreneur means that you will have daily interaction with a variety of people, from employees to vendors to customers to investors.

You must have the ability to effectively manage people without offending (or strangling) them; the ability to haggle over price with vendors without insulting them; the ability to accept good advice from mentors and politely discount the bad without offending them; the ability to overlook mistakes or quickly rectify them; and the one I have trouble with: the ability to tolerate incompetence without losing your cool, at least on the outside.

Playing well with others is something you should have learned in kindergarten. If you didn't learn it then, you certainly don't want to learn it now at the expense of your business.

9. *Do you have financial backing?* The number-one cause of business failure after operator error is a lack of money. Every entrepreneur on the planet (other than me, of course) has at one time or other overestimated revenue and underestimated cost. We're a positive bunch, we entrepreneurs. We just know that the second we hang out our "Open" sign the world is going to beat a path to our door and deluge us with money. Yeah, right. I've never seen a business plan or listened to a business pitch that didn't paint the numbers with a rose-colored brush.

Stop lying to yourself and honestly look at the numbers. You know darn good and well that your lofty revenue projections and bargain-basement cost estimates are about as accurate as a blind monkey's stock picks. Don't gamble your house on numbers you pull out of your ear. Don't fool yourself by thinking, "Everybody will buy my product!" because it just ain't so.

Be realistic. Make sure you have enough money to see you through the first year of operation or until the business can sustain itself. Make sure you double and triple check your estimated cost of doing business.

When it comes to the numbers, the fewer surprises, the better.

10. *Do you have experience in the type of business you plan to start?* This should be a no-brainer, but it never occurs to some people who think they can learn a business as they go.

If you can't locate your car's engine you have no business buying a Lube-N-Go franchise.

If you don't know your salami from your baloney it would be lunacy to open a sub shop.

The most successful business owners have prior experience in the industry in which they have set up shop. Unfortunately, many entrepreneur wannabes aren't willing to put in the grunt time required to get the experience that would make their transition to the big game much smoother and much less risky.

If you're thinking about buying a Subway franchise, go work at a Subway for a few months to learn how the business works from the inside out. After you're up to your elbows in pickles and onions for awhile you may find slinging subs is not for you.

If you're thinking about starting a dry cleaning business, go get a job at a dry cleaner. If you think owning a restaurant would be cool, go bus tables or work in the kitchen of a restaurant to make sure it's the best business for you. Get the worst job you can because as an owner-operator chances are it's a job you'll have to do occasionally when employees call in sick.

I really don't know why, other than I was a fan of the old TV show *Cheers*, but I've always wanted to own a neighborhood pub. You know, a little hole-in-the-wall place where all my pals could hang out and everybody knows your name. Then I remember that I know nothing about the bar business. Then I remember that I don't even drink and don't like to associate with people who do. Then I realize that all my pals would expect to drink there for free and I'd be ticked off about it and they wouldn't be pals very long. Eventually I'd be left alone in my bar sipping hot milk and lamenting my choice of business venture.

Even knowing what I know about business in general, do you think I'd be a success in the bar business? Probably not. Just because I know how to lift a glass to my lips doesn't mean I'm qualified to run a bar. Just because I wear shoes doesn't mean I should open a shoe store. Just because I love hamburgers doesn't mean I should start a catsup business. You get the drift.

"But , Tim, I don't want to work in my business," you might say. "I just want to own it and let someone else run it. Why should I waste my time working in an industry when I can find a great manager to handle everything for me?"

Let me tell you something, Bubba, absentee ownership, in most cases, is a cocktail recipe for disaster. If you don't want to run the business you will have to find someone who does, and do you really want to bet the success of your business on the actions of someone else?

What if the person you found to run your business runs it into the ground and you're left to pick up the pieces and have no clue what to do? What if your perfect manager realizes that they are so good at running your business they should be running one of their own? They can just open up shop across the street and drive you out of business before you know what hits you.

I don't care what business you're considering, your chances of success are far greater if you've got experience in the industry, period.

Bonus Question: Have You Ever Started a Business Before?

Prior business ownership is not a prerequisite to business success, but it sure can't hurt. Many successful entrepreneurs have the skeletons of past businesses hidden in their closet; this means that many first, second, and even third businesses fail. It's how you handle the failure that determines your odds for future success.

I've started a lot of businesses and most of them succeeded, but a few of the early ones didn't. I failed several times before finally succeeding and that's okay. We all have to start somewhere and we all fail. The key is to fail quickly and cheaply, so you can learn your lesson with minimal damage to your ego and bank account.

If this is your first business you should do everything you can to minimize the damage of potential failure just in case. Bootstrap as much as possible. Keep costs and overhead at a minimum. Don't bet the farm until it looks like the odds are in your favor.

Do as much as you can yourself so you don't have to pay someone else to do it. And the biggie: Keep your day job until the business can support you at the level of income you require. Notice I didn't say the level you *desire*, I said the level you *require*—two completely different things. When you're bootstrapping a business you also need to bootstrap your personal life. That may require that you cut expenses and put your family on a budget. You can't pay yourself a huge salary if there's not enough money in the bank to keep the lights on. You should be plowing every dollar of profit back into the business, not pulling them out to pay for extravagances at home.

I learned a lot of things from those early failed ventures that I used to succeed later on. I learned the value of planning and good money management. I learned the importance of providing great customer service. I learned lessons on dealing with vendors who failed to deliver and customers who failed to pay and employees who failed to show up. With every setback came a lesson learned. That's how I became a business expert, my friend, by making every mistake in the book and learning something from every last one of them.

As Gomer Pyle would say, "Fool me once, shame on you. Fool

me twice, shame on me." I rarely make the same mistake twice. I also rarely quote Gomer Pyle.

Business is a lot like marriage: You learn a lot of things on the first one that may come in handy the second or third time around.

You can see why I didn't become a marriage counselor.

So, back to our test; how did you score?

Give yourself 1 point for every "Yes" answer and zero points for every "No." If your score totals 5 or better, you just might have what it takes to start your own business.

If your answers lean heavily to the "No" side, you're probably better off working for someone else, at least till you can tip the score in your favor.

Now that you've passed or failed my completely unscientific personality test with flying or dismal colors, let's talk about the skills that can make the business road less bumpy for you.

There are a variety of skills that will come in handy as an entrepreneur and chances are you do not possess them all and that's okay. One of the great things about being an entrepreneur is that even if you lack certain skills (and we all do) you can always partner with someone or hire employees with those skills to help round out your company skill set.

Also keep in mind that different stages of business require different skills. It's kind of like going fly fishing. The further out in the water you go the deeper your waders should be. Just try not to end up with a carp in your pants. Here we go.

People Skills

We touched on this earlier, but it's a biggie so let's beat this dead horse a little more. Unless your business is one where you never have to interact with humans, you must have good people skills to succeed. That's not to say that you can't be a total idiot or a complete ass and still succeed in business, but that is the exception rather than the rule. Unless your business idea is so groundbreaking that it greatly overshadows the entrepreneur behind it, you're going to need good people skills to succeed.

Remember, in the beginning you will probably be the first contact people have with your business. And people do business with people they like. When people like you they want you to succeed, your happiness is important to them, and they become mentally invested in your success.

You could have a product that the customer desperately needs, but if the customer doesn't like you personally or fails to have confidence in you, they will buy the product from someone else.

My friend, author and speaker Bob Sommers, calls it "the likeability factor" and in my opinion it's one of the biggest reasons businesses pass or fail. If you can't sell yourself first, you won't get much chance to sell your product later.

Networking/Socializing Skills

How many times have you heard someone say, "It's not what you know; it's who you know"?

In business you can take that line to the bank because it is absolutely true. I can't tell you how many times a casual conversation has led to a business deal that put money in my pocket. Or how often a person who himself didn't need my product or service has referred me to a friend of a friend of a friend who ended up being a customer.

A successful entrepreneur should also be a successful schmoozer. It's the entrepreneurial equivalent of kissing babies and shaking hands. Whether it's the weekly Rotary luncheon or a Chamber function or a trade show or a convention, show up with a pocketful of business cards and meet as many people as you can.

And don't just save your socializing skills for the big functions with dozens of people. Always be on the lookout for the opportunity to meet new people one-on-one. Grab every chance you get to strike up a conversation and hand out your card. When you're sitting in the departure area of the airport, when you're in the waiting room at the doctor's office, when you're at a restaurant having lunch, when you're watching your kid play soccer, chances to strike up conversations and expand your business abound.

You never know when the guy sitting next to you on the plane may know someone who needs exactly what you're selling. Or when that nice lady standing in the buffet line ahead of you at the church picnic turns out to be the buyer for a chain of department stores.

Smile, be nice, make chit-chat. Jeez, did I really just say that?

Leadership Skills

To be an entrepreneur is to be a leader. Even if you are a company of one, you must have the skills to take charge and lead when it comes to your clients. I've seen many a sales meeting go to heck in a hand basket because the entrepreneur making the presentation didn't take charge of the room and get his message across to the customer.

It's much easier to learn leadership skills when you have only yourself to manage, so buy some books on leadership now and stock up your brain for the future. Read biographies of great leaders. Learn the skills they used to motivate and practice them yourself. These skills will come in very handy as you add employees and your business grows.

Always lead by example, not by rule. In other words, do not attempt to lead with a "do as I say and not as I do" mentality. Your employees will see right through that smokescreen and see you not as a leader, but as "the boss." And what an ugly word *boss* is. Everybody hates their boss. Nobody wants to be bossed around. Nobody likes being called "bossy." Boss is not a term of respect. If you like being called boss you're an egotistical ass, not an entrepreneur.

To me, *boss* is one of the most insulting things an employee could ever call me. If someone calls me boss I know that they see me not as a figure of respect, motivation, and inspiration, but as a figure of domination and dictatorship.

I do not want to lord over my employees, and if being respected as a person and as the business owner is important to you, you should avoid being "the boss" at all cost. No one willingly follows a boss, but everyone will follow a leader.

Management Skills

You can manage your checkbook, you can manage your hair, and you can manage your kid's soccer team, but can you really manage a business?

Business management skills encompass a wide variety of tasks, including managing the daily operation, growth, employees, customer relations, investor relations, and so on. Poor managers make for poor entrepreneurs.

Employee Relations Skills

Your employees can be one of the most important assets your business can have. Good employees can help build a business while bad employees can help tear it down. Good employees are hard to find and it's important to keep them happy.

Every employee should feel needed and appreciated and know that they are a key part of the team. Prove that to them often with personal admiration and rewards. Believe it or not, a pat on the back is more important than a $100 bonus to some people.

Get to know your employees; understand what motivates them and makes them tick. Keep the relationship friendly, but professional. There should never be any doubt about who's in charge. In a later chapter we'll talk more about the relationship you should have with your employees.

Team-Building Skills

As your organization grows you must have the ability to build a team that can take your business to the next level. Your team includes not only your staff but also your family, partners, accountant, attorney, and investors.

Anyone who has the ability to impact your bottom line and growth should be part of your team. It will be important for you to have the ability to identify and recruit those who can help your cause. You must be able to get them excited about your vision and to get them emotionally or financially invested in your dream.

Marketing and Sales Skills

Until you grow your business to the point that you can justify adding a marketing and sales person, it will be up to you to come up with ways to market your business. Marketing is one of the most critical areas of business and getting the word out to customers is the first step in generating revenue. If you fail to market, the business will fail to exist.

Like marketing, selling is vital to the success of your business. Starting out you will probably be the one making sales calls and closing deals for your business. You must have the ability to sit in front of a prospective client and sell them on your service or product.

Many entrepreneurs find this difficult to do as sales is more art than skill. This is also why one of your first hires when able should be a good salesperson.

Time-Management Skills

Unfortunately, there are only so many hours in the day and for entrepreneurs that means we must manage our time well or inevitably some things won't get done.

I find that it helps to plan your day the night before. I know before I ever get to the office what I have to do that day. And I know the order I will do things in. Of course, something always comes up to throw a monkey wrench in my plan. When the unexpected happens I try to add it to the next day's schedule. If that's not possible, I deal with it and then try to get back on track. That's not always possible, but having a plan certainly helps.

Do you currently have all these skills? Probably not. Very few people possess them all even after years in business.

Does a lack of these skills mean that you shouldn't start your own business? Not at all.

Entrepreneurial skills can be learned and improved over time, and as I said earlier, you can find partners and employees to plug the holes you leave open.

Just look at me. Do you think I've always been so perfect?

Heck no. Just ask my wife.

CHAPTER 14

There Are No Dumb Business Questions, Only Dumb Business Question Askers

"Can I ask you a dumb question," I'm often asked.

"Sure," I reply, "if you don't mind me giving you a dumb answer."

Writing an advice column, whether it be advice for love or money or business, is sometimes hard to do with a straight face. Occasionally a question comes over the digital transom that just makes me go, "Huh?"

It's kind of like trying to stifle a giggle when Granny breaks wind at Sunday dinner. Some things are just better left ignored. Of course, it's hard to blame a dumb business question on the dog.

After years of writing a small business advice column I've decided there really is no such thing as a dumb business question, but there sure are a lot of dumb business question askers, bless their hearts.

Like the e-mail from the guy who had such a great business idea that he was afraid to tell anyone about it because he was sure they'd steal it. He was curious why he was having a hard time getting anyone to invest in an idea he refused to share with them.

Most of the requests for advice I receive are sincere and intelligent, and as a sincere and (somewhat) intelligent columnist, I always feel obligated to dispense the best advice I can for the betterment of the person who asked the question. However, once in a while a real stinker hits the old in-box and it takes everything I've got to resist shooting back an answer that is worthy of the question asked.

In other words, when I get a dumb question, my gut reaction is to respond with an answer of equal intelligence, or the lack thereof. Something subtle, like:

"Dear Bob,

Forget starting your own business. The best thing you can do for mankind is to go find a really sharp pair of scissors, hold them to your chest, and run . . . really fast . . . in heavy traffic."

To quote that great entrepreneur savant Forrest Gump: Stupid is as stupid does. Greater words of wisdom have rarely been offered before or since.

Then I remember that as an advice columnist I have a duty to my readers, my editor, my publisher, and above all, to my family, who enjoy eating on a regular basis. There aren't too many openings for smart aleck writers anymore (darn that Dave Barry), so I bite my tongue and respond to the question as intelligently as I can. It's not as satisfying as firing off a sarcastic retort, but it is much better on the old bank account.

The following are real questions from real people who are running around loose among us. If you recognize your question, please don't be offended. This is all in good fun, and remember, ridicule is the sincerest form of flattery. Or something like that.

Here's a question I get at least once a week: "I have never been in business before, but I think I'd be really good at it. Can you tell me what would be the best business for me to start?"

Hmm . . . how about one that involves the Psychic Hotline, since that's who I will have to consult to answer your question. I don't know anything about you or your background or your abilities or your talents or your experience or anything else. How can I possibly tell you what would be the best business for you? Who do I look like, Miss Cleo?

Here's one of my favorites: "I need to make a lot of money really, really fast, like, by Friday. What business should I start?"

I have one word for you, my friend: counterfeiting.

Somebody hand me an umbrella. It's raining stupid in here.

Here's an oldie but a goodie: "I have a killer business idea, but I don't have any money. Do you ever invest in businesses and if so, can you send the money in cash?"

Unfortunately, I invest only in nonlethal business ideas, so I'll have to pass on your killer idea. Thanks for thinking of me, though.

The moron window is now closed. Thank you, drive through.

And my all-time favorite: "I have a great product, but I can't get anybody to buy it. How can I make customers buy my product?"

How can you *make* a customer buy your product? Heck I don't know. Maybe hold their dog hostage or twist their arm till they cry uncle and whip out their checkbook? Or do what I did with my kids when they were little: Threaten to put them in time out if they don't buy something from you right this second!

Don't make me get up and sell you something, young man . . .

I could go on, but I think the point is made.

Keep those cards and letters coming, boys and girls.

It's readers like you that make this job so darn interesting.

CHAPTER 15

Start Your Business When Life Tells You To, Never Before

When I first approached the business editor at my local news-paper with the idea for what would become my weekly column, *Small Business Q&A with Tim Knox*, he keenly observed, "You seem to be pretty busy running all these businesses. Given your schedule, are you sure you have the time to write a column every week?"

Never being one to let a valid concern get in the way of my ambitions, I boldly answered, "No sweat. I could write a column every day, that's how much I have to say."

Boy, was I glad he didn't take me up on that one. Writing a regular newspaper column is one of the hardest tasks I've ever tackled, but even through the periods of writer's block and the occasional missed deadline, it continues to be one of my favorite things to do.

Now, three years later, I've written more than 150 columns on entrepreneurship and small business, and rarely have I run out of fodder for the advice mill because each column is based either on my own experiences as an entrepreneur and consumer or on questions submitted by readers.

I like writing about my own misadventures (every day is an adventure in my world), but I have often found that the questions I get from readers offer far more lessons on business than my own daily deeds. These questions cover a wide variety of business and entrepreneurship topics and come from people in all walks of life, in all professions, in all situations, with full and limited mental capacity (bless their hearts).

My best advice has been dispensed to these folks over the years and that's why I'm including a few of their questions in this book. They will help introduce topics that I think are important to anyone involved in business or management. They are like mental Viagra, and couldn't we all use a nice shot of that every once in a while?

I also think it's important that you know that you are not alone in the big, cruel business world; there are others out there with the same questions and concerns that you have when it comes to your business.

So let's begin with a question from a young man by the name of Carlton who had a business degree in hand, but didn't really know what to do with it. Sound familiar? It should. I hear from many B-school graduates who have no clue what to do next. They are like dogs who chase cars and when they finally catch one have no idea what to do with it.

That said, you don't have to be a new graduate to relate to Carlton's question. You may be fresh out of high school or in the middle of life or retiring from one career and looking to start the next. The question looms for us all: I want to start my own business; now what?

Here's the letter from Carlton:

Q: Tim, I'm graduating this year with a degree in business and would like to start my own business rather than get a corporate job. I have a few business ideas, but none of them really gets me excited. Should I just put my business plans on hold and get a job until the right opportunity comes along?

A: Congratulations on the impending degree, Carlton. Never having attended a higher institution of learning myself, I have great respect for anyone who can withstand four years of nonmandatory schooling and emerge with sheepskin in hand.

I do have a pair of sheepskin boots. They make me look taller, but I don't think they make me any smarter.

Seriously, I envy your position and applaud your efforts. You're young, you're educated, you're ambitious, you're probably much better looking than me, and soon you'll leave the comfort and warmth of your tiny dorm room to go out into the big, cold, cruel world to seek your fortune and make your mark. The fun is just about to begin, my young friend. I hope you're ready for the ride.

Now on to your question: Should you put your business plans on hold and get a job until the right opportunity comes along? That's a decision that should be made based on your personal situation, your short- and long-term goals, your finances, your responsibilities, your commitments, and all the other factors that make Carlton's world go around.

I can tell you that as a breed, we entrepreneurs are an impatient lot and many of us jump on the first business bandwagon that comes along just for the sake of being in business. That's a mistake that usually comes back to bite us in our entrepreneurial behinds.

Never go into business just because you think that's what you're expected to do. You should always have a solid idea and a very clear plan of action before starting a business. It is the failure to plan that leads to the failure to succeed. You didn't plan on having to work so hard or so many hours, you didn't plan on hating the business you're in, you didn't plan on needing so much money to keep the doors open, you didn't plan on growing so fast or so slow, you didn't plan on there being no market for your product, you didn't plan on losing your house, and so forth. A failure to plan is a plan to fail. Of course you probably learned that in "Old Business Adage 101."

Starting a business simply because you have a business degree is not the smart thing to do. That would be like deciding to jump out of a plane just because someone handed you a parachute.

Start your business career only when you get an idea or find a business concept that gets you so excited and so passionate that you can't sleep at night. That's when you go into startup mode and not a minute before.

Carlton's question is one I hear a lot: When is the right time to go into business? Should I wait until I have a lot of money in the bank? Should I wait until I have all my debts paid off? Should I wait until my kids are grown? Should I wait until I retire? Should I wait until my spouse says it's okay? Should I wait until the planets align just so and the voice of God echoes in that empty space between my ears?

The truth is there may never be a perfect time in your life to start your business. There will always be reasons why you shouldn't take the leap at that particular moment. There will always be people telling you that you have no right to start a business. There will always be bills that need to be paid and groceries to be bought.

And here is the flipside of the truth coin: If you wait until the time is right, you will never start your business.

There is never a perfect time to start a business. But there is always opportunity to do so. It's up to you to decide when the time is right. And when that time comes it's up to you to grab onto the opportunity and make it work no matter the circumstances.

CHAPTER 16

How Important Are Book Smarts and Experience to Business Success?

Here's another question I get a lot, usually from readers with PhD, MBA, or some other combination of letters after their name: In business, which is more important, education or experience?

Before I reveal my answer, let me ask you a question. Have you seen that wonderful example of reality TV run amok called *Fear Factor*? If you haven't seen it you've probably at least heard about it. *Fear Factor* puts contestants through all sorts of pseudo-death-defying feats like bungee jumping off a bridge over a pool of crocodiles or driving a car through a wall of fire (you know, the stuff we did for fun in high school). The contestant who overcomes their personal fear factor wins the cash and prizes (usually at the cost of their dignity and self-esteem, but hey, such is the price of fame).

The highlight of *Fear Factor* is the eating competition, or should I call it the "shove disgusting stuff in your mouth and try not to gag" contest. That's when contestants are invited to partake of all sorts of culinary fare that we southerners call "bait."

Contestants choke down yummy stuff like earthworms and grubs, live bugs and spiders, moose intestines, old fruitcake (oh, the horror), and my personal favorite, live giant cockroaches, probably from Michigan or New Jersey. At this point the competition becomes not so much who can overcome their fear factor, but who has the lowest gag reflex.

To address the question of which is more important, education or expertise in the world of business, makes me feel a little like those contestants because no matter how I answer I am opening a giant can of worms that I will undoubtedly be forced to eat later.

My highly educated readers and peers will argue that education is much more important than experience, while my pals with more experience than education will argue that time on the job is more important than time spent on the books.

Either way, it's worms à la carte for me.

Oh well, I've eaten more than my share of crow over the years. How much worse can worms be?

It's important to understand that the success of an entrepreneur is not measured by how much education he or she has or how many years of experience are under his or her belt. An entrepreneur's success is best measured by personal satisfaction and achievements, not degrees on a wall or sand through an hourglass.

Let's start with what my Mama would call book smarts (i.e., education). Is a Bachelor's degree or better required to succeed in business? Of course not. An MBA from Harvard might give you a leg up in a job interview and impress the girls at the office party, but it certainly doesn't guarantee that you will succeed in business. Nor does it automatically mean that you will be a better business person than someone who didn't finish high school. There are a lot of college grads who can't even remember what field their degree is in and just as many MBAs flipping burgers instead of businesses.

Knowledge is a good thing only if you know what to do with it.

Perhaps it's the academic environment itself that turns mere mortal nerds into budding entrepreneurs. The late 1990s proved that college students with no experience beyond organizing a frat keg party could start businesses that would exceed all expectations. Many would argue that the key to success for most of these ventures was that the founders (or the venture capitalist financing them) were smart enough to know that while they had an abundance of education, they needed experienced managers to really run the show.

Larry Page and Sergey Brin were college students when they started the company that would become Google. They were smart enough to bring in Eric Schmidt to be chairman and CEO when the business took off. Schmidt was the former CEO of Novell and CTO of Sun Microsystems. A PhD, Schmidt is a man of education and experience.

Jerry Yang and David Filo were candidates in Electrical Engineering at Stanford when they started Yahoo! (Yet Another Hierarchical Officious Oracle) in 1994. They brought in Tim Koogle from Motorola to run things shortly thereafter and now the company is led by Terry Semel, who previously spent 24 years running Warner Bros.

Now on to experience. Is experience a precursor of business success? Not on your life. You could have 30 years of successful experience as an industry executive and bomb as an entrepreneur in the same industry. Even experienced entrepreneurs aren't guaranteed success in every venture. When it comes to succeeding in business too many other factors come into play besides years on the job.

So, when it comes to succeeding in business, which is more important: education or experience? While neither is as helpful as a rich relative and a market that's starving for a product, both education and experience can play a large part in business success, but neither outweighs the other on the scales of success.

Can you succeed in business without one or the other, or even without both? You bet. Can I get ketchup with those worms?

Many successful entrepreneurs began with no experience and no college credits to their name. Talent, ambition, drive, creativity, determination, and good old-fashioned hard work have fueled many business careers, including my own.

A combination of education and experience (and a variety of other things) is the best recipe for success. As the old saying goes, "There is no better education than that which comes from experience."

In the end, it really doesn't matter how much education or experience you have. It's what you do with it that matters.

CHAPTER 17

Are You Ever Too Old to Start Your Own Business?

I read the other day that thanks to advances in modern medicine and preventive healthcare people are living longer than ever before. I personally think that the drug Viagra started this new trend. No, Viagra itself will not make you live longer, but if men think they can have sex well into their seventies and eighties they will hold on for dear life.

There's nothing more inspirational to an 80-year-old man than a lifetime refill of Viagra.

A healthy white female is now expected to live into her eighties and a healthy white male is expected to live until his 80-year-old wife decides she's had enough of the old boy and lays him out with a frying pan.

I tell everyone that my wife is killing me slowly, but that's a story for another time.

I know many of you with rich uncles hate to hear that people are living longer, but it's true. And since we humans live and die by our statistics ("The man on Oprah said I could live to be 100 and by God Oprah wouldn't let him say it if it wasn't true!"), it is only natural that seniors remain active and productive long past the traditional retirement age of 65.

Living longer has thrown a huge monkey wrench into the plans of a lot of seniors who expected their retirement money to carry them through till it was time to shuffle off this mortal coil. Many are now worried that their golden years will be spent living on crackers and Alpo instead of munching on the good life.

This is one reason why I'm hearing from a lot of seniors who want to know if I think they are too old for a ride on the rickety old business rollercoaster. They're certainly tall enough to ride this ride, but are they ever too old?

Here's my standard answer to this and most other questions: It depends. I have to be honest that on more than one occasion using the word "depends" when talking to a senior citizen confused the issue, but I'm quick to qualify my answer before we get off on a discussion of bladder control undergarments.

It depends on your health, your energy, your drive, your goals, and of course, your finances. If all those are in good shape and you have your spouse's approval (that's a biggie on the depends meter), then there is absolutely no reason why you should not start a business at any age.

In fact, the numbers are actually in your favor. According to recent studies, 22 percent of men and 14 percent of women over 65 are self-employed. That's compared to just 7 percent for other age groups.

According to a 2003 Vanderbilt University study, the number of entrepreneurs age 45 to 64 was expected to grow by 15 million by 2006. That was compared to an expected decline of 4 million entrepreneurs age 25 to 44.

A 1998 survey of baby boomers conducted by the American Association of Retired Persons (AARP) revealed that 80 percent of respondents planned to work beyond retirement age, and 17 percent of those planned to launch new businesses.

The study noted, "Self-employment among American workers increases with age, with the most dramatic jump occurring at age 65."

Older entrepreneurs may also find starting a business easier than their younger counterparts because older entrepreneurs tend to have more experience to draw from and more assets with which to finance a business.

Further evidence comes from a report released by Barclays Bank entitled, "Third Age Entrepreneurs—Profiting from Experience."

The report showed that older entrepreneurs are responsible for 50 percent more business startups than 10 years ago. This amounts to around 60,000 business startups last year alone. The survey also showed that today's third age entrepreneurs (as the report calls entrepreneurs over the age of 50) don't mind putting in the hours required to build their business. Nearly 49 percent work an average of 36 hours or more a week.

Third-agers, as they're called, also rated holidays, lack of stress, and a balance between work and home life more important than their younger counterparts.

The report further showed that only 27 percent run the business as the only source of household income, with 51 percent supplementing their pension.

Other key findings showed that third age startups account for 15 percent of all new businesses, and third age entrepreneurs are three times more likely to be male than female.

There are wrinkles when it comes to older entrepreneurship (sorry, couldn't resist). Many businesses fail within the first few years and older entrepreneurs may be less able to handle the financial loss than younger entrepreneurs. It's one thing to lose everything at 25, but it's a much bigger deal to be financially ruined at 65.

So my advice to my older peers is that if your health and finances allow (and the spouse gives the green light), by all means start your business and have yourself a ball.

Climb on the entrepreneurial rollercoaster and hang on tight.

You get the senior discount, by the way.

Just try not to lose your lunch when things get bumpy and you'll probably do just fine.

And for your own sake, take it easy on the Viagra, will you? You're not 29 anymore.

CHAPTER 18

Look Out Boys, Them Crazy Girls Are Catching Up!

I had the honor of speaking recently at a women's business association luncheon on the topic of entrepreneurship. When I mentioned to my wonderful, adoring, supportive wife the day before that I would be speaking to a group of women entrepreneurs, she asked, "Why on earth would they ask you to speak?"

When I feigned hurt feelings (men do have feelings, we just don't use them, or use the word "feigned" for that matter), she waved a hand at me and said, "My point is, what in the world can a man tell a roomful of women that they don't already know?"

Henny Youngman, Ralph Cramden, Rodney Dangerfield, Tim Knox. At least I'm in good company.

But she had a point. What the heck did I know about women in business? I had stumbled into a Victoria's Secret once by mistake (I swear) and just about died of embarrassment when a saleswoman caught me chatting up one of the mannequins.

I did discover Victoria's Secret, however: She is not a nice girl.

So as not to look like a total idiot in front of this group of what I now call "womentrepreneurs," I decided to do a little research on the topic.

Here's what I discovered: While some still believe business is a man's world, the women are making some pretty good strides in the race with the good old boys.

It reminds me of the time me and a bunch of my idiot buddies raided the girl's locker room just as the girl's softball team was coming in from practice. I don't know if you've ever felt the wrath of a bunch of bat-wielding, cleat-wearing, ticked off female softball players, but to quote my friend Eddie Ray Mason, "Run faster boys, them crazy girls are catching up!"

According to the Center for Women's Business Research, there are over 10 million women-owned businesses in the United States, employing 18 million people and generating $2.32 trillion in sales.

Women start businesses at two times the rate of men and women-owned businesses account for 28 percent of all businesses in the United States and represent about 775,000 new startups per year and account for 55 percent of new startups.

In the past 25 years the number of women-owned firms in the United States has doubled, employment has increased fourfold, and their revenues have risen fivefold.

One thing that I found particularly interesting was that the top growth industries for women-owned businesses in recent years were construction, wholesale trade, transportation/communications, agribusiness, and manufacturing, industries traditionally dominated by men. Dang, boys, what's next—Victoria's Backhoe Supply?

Here is the question I sought particularly to answer: Given the difference in the way men and women approach most things, do women approach business differently than men? I've been compared to a bull in a china shop when it comes to business. Would a female counterpart approach things differently? More gracefully, perhaps? With a little more feeling and a little less bravado?

As my lovely bride would say, "Duh."

In her book, *How to Run Your Business Like a Girl*, Elizabeth Cogswell Baskin explored common female traits and how women entrepreneurs—and perhaps men, as well—can use those traits to their entrepreneurial advantage.

Baskin reported that women tend to use three unique strengths more than their male counterparts: trusting their intuition, focusing on relationships, and putting more emphasis on keeping their life in balance.

Women trust their gut. Women are much more likely to make a decision based on a gut feeling. Women may gather the facts and figures necessary to back up that feeling, but they generally know what they want to do based on intuition.

Women build strong relationships. Men play the game of business like a sport. They are out to win and dominate. "Women," Baskin says, "are much more interested in establishing a connection."

Women find a balance between work and life. A number of women interviewed for this book cited quality of life as their reason for starting a business, alluding to their desire to find a way to juggle family and work. "If having more time for your family is important to you, find a way to work that into your day. It's not so much how much work you do, but being able to decide when you'll do it."

Baskin offers one more piece of advice to women in the early stages of their business:

You don't have to know everything. My wife would argue this point because she really does know everything, but Baskin says when it comes to business, thinking you know everything is not the key to success.

"It's amazing how many women say they didn't know anything when they started their business," Baskin said. "Don't be afraid to ask for help—you don't have to be perfect at everything."

Solid business advice, for guys and gals.

CHAPTER 19

How to Choose the Business That's Right for You

One of the first questions every fledgling entrepreneur asks is, How do I choose the business that's right for me? To which I always reply: Beats me, Bubba. That's like asking me what you should be when you grow up. Heck, I don't even know what I want to be when I grow up, so how am I supposed to predict your future?

You are wise to ask the question, however, because many entrepreneurs dive into business without giving much thought to the correlation between their happiness and the industry they've chosen.

I always compare starting a business to jumping into a pool of freezing water. There are typically two types of entrepreneurs who take the plunge.

The first are the "Toe Testers." These are those cautious folks who just stick their big toe in the pool to gauge the temperature of the water. It is for these careful entrepreneurs that the phrase "testing the waters" was coined.

Toe Testers enter the business pool slowly, a little bit at a time. The lesson to be learned from Toe Testers is to start slowly and don't feel like you have to wade in too fast. Ease into the business pool gradually to make sure it's right for you. Remember, many entrepreneurs realize that the business world is not right for them only after they are in it up to their necks. And that's when the term "sink or swim" takes on a whole new meaning.

The next type of entrepreneur is the "High Diver." These are those fearless souls who climb the ladder and dive into the business pool head first without worrying about the depth of the water or the dangers that lurk beneath the surface.

It is for these entrepreneurs that the phrase "damn the torpedoes, full speed ahead" was coined. Quite often these entrepreneurial daredevils find themselves drowning in unknown waters or end up with their heads buried in the bottom of the pool.

Both types of entrepreneurs may find success, depending on how well equipped they are to handle the water they are diving into.

Here are a few ideas to help better prepare you for the plunge.

Let your experience be your guide. Start with what you know. If you have spent 20 years working as an accountant or you love to build wooden toy trains as a hobby, consider how you can take that experience and turn it into a successful business.

You might also find a great business idea right under your nose. Look around your workplace. Do you see needs that are going unmet or can you think of a better way of doing something? If so, you might have the seed for a profitable business.

Do what you love and enjoy what you do. I can't emphasize this enough. Many people start a business for the wrong reason: to get rich. While it is true that many millionaires in this country made their fortunes from their own business ventures, that should not be your sole motivation for starting a business. If you don't enjoy what you do, you will not be successful, at least not from a mental point of view. Sure, the monetary rewards can be tremendous, but the mental anguish of working in a business you don't enjoy is a high price to pay. I talk to entrepreneurs all the time who are running successful businesses, but are so unhappy as a result that they literally make themselves sick. If you don't enjoy what you do, the business will become a chore, not a joy.

Don't reinvent the wheel, just make it better. Many first-time entrepreneurs assume that they have to come up with a new business idea to be successful. That simply is not true. Most successful businesses are born not of innovation, but of necessity. Instead of trying to come up with an idea that changes the world, take a look at the world around you and see where there might be a void that needs filling or a business concept that needs improvement.

Many successful businesses have been built by taking a traditional business and making it better. Domino's Pizza was certainly not the first to offer home delivery of pizza, but they were the first to guarantee it would be delivered piping hot to your door in 30 minutes or less. Amazon.com was not the first company to sell books, but they were one of the first that would let you buy books from the comfort of your own home while sitting in your underwear.

Focus on a niche. Many businesses have gone broke trying to be all things to all people. The ability to offer a gazillion products under one roof is all well and good for Wal-Mart, but not for most new small businesses. Try to identify a niche that you would enjoy working in and think about starting a business therein. If you love to work outdoors, consider starting a landscaping business. If you enjoy working with numbers, think about becoming an accountant or CPA. When's the last time you had your gardener do your taxes? You get the idea. Focus on a niche and become an expert in your field.

A franchise might be an option. Many new entrepreneurs consider buying a franchise operation instead of starting a business from scratch. Franchises are a good way to jumpstart the process because they have already done much of the hard work for you. They have proven the business model, established guidelines for running the business, spent millions of dollars on establishing the brand, and so forth.

Buying a franchise is typically a very expensive and involved process that is beyond the scope of this book. The best thumbnail of advice I can give you is to thoroughly investigate the franchisor and the opportunity, use your own attorney to do the deal, and read the fine print in the franchise agreement.

It's hard to swim in a crowded pool. If the business pool is already filled with other companies doing the same thing you want to do, chances are you will fail in the face of established competition. To succeed in such a crowded pool you will have to do something to stand out from the crowd (and I don't mean greeting customers while wearing a bright red Speedo). If you can't quickly and easily differentiate yourself from a large group of competitors, you're better off choosing another business.

Above all, take your time. Whatever business you choose to start, I encourage you to take the time required to make an informed, intelligent decision. Think about starting part time while you still have your current job (and income) to fall back on.

Talk to friends and associates who use the product or service you will provide to see if they would consider becoming paying customers.

Remember, in business you can end up swimming in success or sinking in failure.

The key to your success might just lie in the sensitivity of your big toe.

CHAPTER 20

Just How Big Is Your Really Big Idea?

At least once a week I'm approached by someone who thinks they have the idea for the next business Holy Grail. Each person, bless their hearts, is convinced that their idea is the really big one, the million-dollar idea that no one has ever had before. And each is positive that if I could help them bring their idea to market we'd both be rich beyond our wildest dreams. I'm not sure how I got involved in their brainstorm, but that's the way it usually goes.

Some of them even have a head full of ideas, like the person who sent in the question below.

Q: I want to start my own business. I have tons of business ideas that all sound great to me, but my husband is not so sure. He says that we need to figure out a way to test my ideas to pick the one that has the best chance of succeeding. I'm ready to just pick one and go for it. What is the best way to determine if a business idea really is as good as it sounds?

A: I know you probably don't want to hear this, but your husband is right (first time for everything). Before you pick a business idea and just go for it, you should test the feasibility of your ideas to make sure they really are as good as you think they are.

Every business idea, no matter how good it sounds while bouncing around inside your head, should be put to the test before you invest time and money in its execution. Success lies not in what *you* think of your idea, but in what the buying public will think.

Many entrepreneurs find out too late that the public's opinion of their idea differs greatly from their own. Wasted time and money aside, the last thing you want is to hear "I told you so!" from your husband, so take a deep breath, slow down, and let's look at the ways you can test the true value of your idea.

There are many ways to test an idea's feasibility, though some ways are not nearly as effective or accurate as others. Most people start out by asking everyone they know what they think of their big idea. This is a good way to start the wheels turning because you may get feedback that you have not considered before, but be warned: This is *not* the best way to test the true feasibility of an idea. Never start a business simply based on what your friends and family think.

There are two things that will happen here. First, your mother will tell you what you want to hear and your best friends will be equally kind. No one who really cares for you will want to rain on your parade no matter how insane your parade might be, so take the wisdom you gain here with a hug and a grain of salt.

On the flip side, your co-workers and casual acquaintances will probably tell you the opposite of what they really think. If they think your idea stinks they'll tell you it's great and if they think your idea is great they'll tell you it stinks. Please don't preach to me about human kindness. Human kindness is always bested by human nature and we humans, by nature, are an envious lot. We hate to see anyone doing better than we are doing and we hate to see anyone who has the potential to leave us behind.

Go watch the movie *Envy* with Jack Black and Ben Stiller and consider this: Why would someone who is broke and stuck in a dead-end job with no other prospects want to see you succeed and leave them behind?

They wouldn't. End of story. Thank you, drive through.

Instead of conferring with friends and family you should run your idea past a number of neutral third parties who are knowledgeable about business and will give you an honest opinion.

Contact the local Small Business Administration (SBA) or the Service Corps of Retired Executives (SCORE) offices and ask to speak with someone knowledgeable who has time to listen to your idea (don't run it past the receptionist). Or speak with the small business liaison at the Chamber of Commerce. Or seek out a successful entrepreneur who is willing to listen and give you an honest opinion about your idea.

Just remember, opinions are like belly buttons: Everybody has at least one and they are all different and usually self-serving. Okay, so maybe belly buttons aren't self-serving, but you get the point.

A more accurate way to judge the feasibility of an idea is to create a SWOT analysis, and no, it doesn't involve guys dressed in black who bust through your skylight with guns blazing, though that would be a cool way to test a business idea.

In this case SWOT stands for Strengths, Weaknesses, Opportunities, and Threats. A SWOT analysis will not only help you gauge the feasibility of your idea, but also help you build on your idea's strengths, identify and correct the weaknesses, and spot ways to take advantage of potential opportunities while avoiding potential threats.

Here's how to perform a simple SWOT analysis. On a piece of paper draw a vertical line down the center of the page. Then draw a horizontal line through the center of the vertical line. The paper is now divided into four quadrants. Label the upper left quadrant "Strengths." Label the upper right quadrant "Weaknesses." Label the lower left quadrant "Opportunities" and the lower right quadrant "Threats."

Now fill in each quadrant based on what you see as the strengths, weaknesses, opportunities, and threats of your business idea. You should repeat this process for every idea you have and each quadrant should have something written in. If you can think of no strengths, weaknesses, opportunities, or threats for a particular idea, that means that you do not have enough information to complete the SWOT analysis, which means you also do not have enough information to effectively execute that idea and turn it into a sustaining business.

Strengths are those things that make your idea a strong one.

Strengths can be personal or product-oriented and may include: prior business experience and success; sufficient funding to start the business; having a customer in hand; having a unique product or service to offer; having an established market; and so forth.

Next list all of the weaknesses of your idea. It is important that you are honest with yourself and list as many weaknesses as you can. Don't pretend that your idea doesn't have any weaknesses because every idea does. You will hurt no one but yourself if you pretend that your idea is bulletproof. Weaknesses might include: lack of capital to start the business; lack of business or management experience; a crowded marketplace; large competitors; and so forth.

Opportunities are those things that you can tap into that might fast track your business idea. We talked about opportunities earlier and how smart entrepreneurs seek out new opportunities rather than waiting for opportunities to come to them.

Opportunities might include: a potential partnership with someone who sells products in the same market; a prime storefront location that is coming available; a competitor going out of business, leaving a hole in the market that may be right for you; and so forth.

Threats are those things that threaten the success of your business idea. Threats might include: uncertain marketplace conditions; strong competitors in the market with lower prices; and possible laws or taxes that may impact your idea. Like weaknesses, it is vital that you are honest when it comes to identifying threats.

Once you have filled in all four quadrants, you should have enough information to begin testing the feasibility of your idea. Do the strengths of your idea outweigh the weaknesses or do the weaknesses outweigh the strengths?

Are the opportunities available to you ample or nonexistent?

Are the threats many or few?

Now that you have your thoughts on paper, is your idea really that big or did it just sound that way inside your head?

Yeah, that's what I thought, too.

CHAPTER 21

Learning About Market Research from the Back of a Boat

I've never been much of a fisherman. Sitting in a small boat for hours watching a red and white bobber float atop the water holds about as much interest for me as watching paint dry.

My old man, on the other hand, would rather have fished than breathe. The few times that I went fishing with him as a young boy (before I was old enough to know better), he'd bait my hook with a worm he'd dug up from our garden and drop it in the water and tell me to watch the bobber until a fish pulled it under the surface. The moment I saw the bobber go under I was to jerk the line and reel the fish in.

I can remember staring at that bobber until my eyes crossed and never, not once, did it ever go under the surface. I am probably the only male child ever born in the great state of Alabama who never caught a single fish. It is but one of the disappointments my ancestors have endured on my account, I assure you.

My old man's bobber, on the other hand, would be jerked under the water within minutes of being tossed in. He'd be catching fish left and right and I'd be sitting there like some angler savant just staring at my bobber and wishing I was old enough to cuss out loud.

I discovered a few years later that the reason he caught all the fish was that he baited his hook with live worms while hanging the dead ones on mine. His worm would wiggle seductively to attract every fish within a two mile radius while mine couldn't even get the attention of a starving turtle if it had swum directly into my hook.

I'm sure I suffered some permanent psychological damage as a result of his actions, but we all have our scars to bear. Mine just happens to be in the shape of a hook with a dead worm hanging from it. The memory has been filed away deep in my psyche in a drawer labeled, "Gee, thanks Dad." It's a drawer I'm sure we all have—mine is probably just a little fuller than most.

While he could have used a few lessons on child rearing, the old man was an expert in one thing that we entrepreneurs often botch or ignore and that is market research. He didn't call it that, of course. He simply said, "Son, never fish in a dry hole."

Let me translate that tidbit of Forrest Gump advice: When flushed through the coherency filter, "don't fish in a dry hole" becomes don't try to sell a product in a market where there are no buyers.

If there are no buyers (hungry fish), there is no market. You can have the greatest product in the world, but if there is no market for your product you might as well pack it up and go dig worms.

Over the years the old man had surveyed every inch of that lake and as a result knew his market well. Through many hours of research he knew exactly where the best customers (i.e., the hungry fish) were in the lake. And that's where he anchored his boat— smack dab in the middle of his own starving niche market.

Having found his hungry market, he tested products to sell into it. He tried crickets, dough balls, lures, worms, and who knows what else, to determine the kind of bait the fish liked best. In the Internet marketing business we call it split testing: offering customers variations on a theme to see which one brings the greatest response.

In his case worms were the product that his market liked best, so that's what he fed them.

He also knew his customers well. He knew that if they liked the product they'd be quick to bite. He knew without flinching exactly how to react when they nibbled the bait. He didn't jerk the line because he knew that might let his customer get away. He tugged it gently until he had his fish hooked, then he'd reel them in and close the deal.

And being the consummate fisherman cum entrepreneur, he always took his best customers to dinner, literally.

What the old man knew was that in fishing, as in business, you succeed by giving customers (be they human or be they fish) what *they* are hungry for, what *they* want or need—not by trying to catch them with the bait or sell them products *you* think they should have.

Sometimes we entrepreneurs think we're smarter than our customers (okay, sometimes we are). We think that they will buy whatever we put in front of them if we just do a really good job of selling it. I've actually heard some arrogant entrepreneurs say, "They'll buy what I have to sell or they can take their business elsewhere." That line of thinking guarantees that you will spend most of your time watching bobbers that never get pulled under.

It's when we take our customers' wants and needs for granted that we fail as entrepreneurs and our lines sit in the water undisturbed.

The problem often comes when entrepreneurs put the cart before the horse.

They will create a product or service for which there is no market.

They fail to survey the market for buyers hungry for the product they have to sell. Instead they grab the bait they think will work and off they go. Usually they come back empty handed.

It happens to entrepreneurs and fishermen all the time.

Let's go back to my fishing story for a moment and talk about other lessons learned. Remember, I found out why the old man always caught a boatload of fish while his pitiful excuse for a son never got a single bite; he would hang the dead worms on my hook and the lively wigglers on his. In business we call that "getting the competitive advantage."

He would direct me to cast my line in waters that he knew were barren while he cast his line in waters teeming with fish. In business we call that "knowing your market."

He would turn to me every so often and say, "Look, Son, I've hooked another one! That makes eight for me in the last ten minutes. How many have you caught? None? Gee, that's too bad."

In business we call that "creating a monopoly."

There were times I recall sitting in that tiny boat with him and his big string of fish on one end and me and my empty string on the other, that I imagined myself picking up an oar and giving it a swing to see how far I could knock him out of the boat.

In business we call that "customer satisfaction."

I mentioned that the old man had surveyed every square inch of that lake over the years and knew exactly where the fish were hiding.

In business we call that "conducting market research," and if your business is new or contemplating a move into new markets, failing to conduct market research could leave you sitting in the boat with no customers nibbling at your hook.

Why conduct market research? The most obvious answer is to verify that there really is a market for your product or service and to determine if the market will support your efforts. A market should be large, easy to reach, and have lots of disposable cash.

A market should be hungry for and passionate about the product you are trying to sell. Otherwise you will find yourself trying to build a business that caters to a market of disinterested, broke people. Like selling house plants to homeless people, that's not a good idea.

Many entrepreneurs make the mistake of giving consideration to their product first, without worrying about who will buy the product when it's done. They come up with a great idea that they are sure the world will love without bothering to ask the world its opinion. They pour thousands of hours and tens of thousands of dollars into their great idea only to end up asking, "Now who will buy my wonderful new widget? Hello? Anybody out there?"

The old man taught me that you should find a pond full of hungry fish first, then come up with the bait to catch them, not vice versa.

Remember, you succeed by giving customers what *they* want or need, not by trying to sell them what *you* think they want or need. Identify a market first, develop the product second. Never put a dime into product creation until you are sure there is a market that will give you a dollar or more for every dime you spend. Never go on instinct and never trust your gut. More often than not you'll find that the great idea you have churning in the pit of your stomach is just gas, and not the kind that will make you money.

Fortunately it has never been easier to conduct market research. Thanks to the Internet you can thoroughly research a market with a few keystrokes. Most industries have associations that publish statistics about their market.

The government publishes enough industry data to choke a horse. You can use online directories and business research tools to gather data. You can also use search engines like Google and Overture (Yahoo!) to search the Web for market data and gather competitive intelligence.

Visit forums and newsgroups to see what people in the industry are talking about. What problems are they complaining about? What needs do they have that are not being met? What itch do they have that you can scratch?

You should also research the competition in the market you are considering. You can learn a great deal from your competitors, such as: What are the top product lines in the market, what is the demand for goods, what are the price points, what is the range in quality, what are they doing that you can do better? And if you find there are no competitors in the market, take that as a red flag. A lack of competition usually means a lack of market. Rarely does a product come along that is so revolutionary that it creates an entirely new market-place, so keep that in mind as you do your research.

I'll say it one more time for those of you who haven't been paying attention: At the end of the day, business, like fishing, is all about finding a pond full of hungry fish and coming up with the best bait to use to catch them.

He who reels in the most customers wins the game.

CHAPTER 22

Perceived Value Is in the Eye of the Beholder

My lovely wife is addicted to yardsales. Every Saturday morning during the summer she bolts out of bed at the crack of dawn and, with a crumpled map in one hand and a wad of dollar bills that could choke a horse in the other, out the door she goes. It matters not that we already have a barn full of our own junk that needs to be dealt with. In her demented mind you can never have enough junk, or as she calls them, "wonderful yardsale finds."

I don't think it says anywhere in the Bible, "She who has the most yardsale finds wins the keys to the kingdom of Heaven," but you can't tell that to my wife. And since a good many of the yardsales held around our area are put on by churches, I guess I can't argue with her, either.

"Hey, Pastor, how much do you want for this lovely set of collection plate dinnerware?"

Over the years she has spent thousands of dollars feeding the yardsale monkey that lives on her back, but it does me no good to bring up the subject of how much money she has spent. It has been explained to me that it is not how much you spend at a yardsale that matters; it is how much you talk them down. In other words, if my dear wife wasn't such an adept haggler, I'd be delivering pizzas at night to help support her ugly habit.

I have tried to get help for her. I found a 12-step program for yardsale junkies and gave her their phone number. She called them up and talked them down to eight steps. I have to hand it to her—she is a pro.

One thing my wife is very good at is telling you exactly what something is worth, especially if it is sitting on a table in your front yard. She can look at a 55-gallon drum of Beanie Babies and tell you within a buck or two what you'll get for the whole lot. She can lay her hands on a set of Elvis Presley commemorative plates or a set of NASCAR bath towels and tell you almost to the penny what such treasures will bring.

As if that weren't enough, she can look at your husband or boyfriend and tell you if he's worthless or not. When it comes to product pricing and perceived value, she is quite a gifted woman, my wonderful wife.

Product pricing is also one of my favorite topics, mainly because no one other than Melissa has a clue how to really go about it, so when I toss out my opinions I sound much smarter than I really am.

Many entrepreneurs just take what the competition charges and cut the price by a few percent. Others who think their product is far superior to the competition may set a higher price and promote themselves on quality. Both are imperfect strategies, but you have to start somewhere.

So what is the best way to determine the perfect price and what is the rule of thumb for raising prices later on?

Like the perfect man, the perfect plan, and the perfect murder (not sure what those three have in common, but there is a link there somewhere), there is no such thing as the perfect price.

There is that mythical price that gives the customer excellent bang for his buck and the company excellent profits for its efforts, but even that price point can't be considered the perfect price. That's called compromise, not perfection.

One popular way to establish a price is to use what I call "The David Copperfield Method," named after the famous magician who made the Statue of Liberty disappear on national TV. The Copperfield Method of product pricing simply means that you pull the price out of thin air. This is similar to the pricing model established by famous entrepreneur Seymour Butt, inventor of the reversible thong, but that's a story for another time. Let's just say that pulling the price out of thin air or a body cavity is not recommended and admitting to such acts looks very bad in a business plan, but I digress.

Believe it or not, pulling the price out of thin air (or other places) is the method that many companies seem to be using these days to establish pricing. It's also the reason many companies disappear. And stink while they're in business.

Pricing is an important aspect of every business because price is used to create financial projections, establish a breakeven point, and calculate profit and loss. Though price may be determined by any number or combination of factors, basically there are three ways to establish the price for your product.

The first way to determine price is to perform a comparative analysis on similar products sold by competitors. Are the features and benefits of their product similar to yours? If so, use the price of the competing product as a possible price point for your product. If your product is superior in quality, features, and benefits, then you might be able to justify a higher price and still be competitive. If your product is inferior, then your price point will be less.

The second way to establish pricing is to calculate the total cost to produce and deliver your product, then figure in an acceptable margin of profit to calculate the final price.

Pricing methods aside, it's important to note that more often than not, product pricing comes down to one thing: perception.

Perception, or as it is more commonly referred to in business, perceived value, is one factor that most entrepreneurs use to determine product pricing. As entrepreneurs, our products are our children. We create them, we nurture them, we grow them, and we love them. And often we perceive their value to be much greater than the market perceives it to be.

It's all about the perception of value.

What makes a $10,000 Rolex watch more valuable than a $100 Timex? In their most basic form both are watches and both perform the exact same function: They tell time. Why then does one sell for a thousand times more than the other? Don't give me that hogwash about superior craftsmanship and quality and longevity.

It's all about perceived value, nothing more.

An expensive wristwatch cannot make you better looking, smarter, healthier, or more popular with the opposite sex. But the perception is that if you have a Rolex on your wrist you must have something going for you that the wearer of a $100 Timex does not.

That perception may or may not be true. There are a lot of broke losers who wear Rolex watches and drive Mercedes convertibles and wear Gucci shoes and Armani suits, not because they can afford it but because the perceived value of these items makes their own perceived value go up.

A Rolex watch for $10,000.

A Mercedes convertible for $110,000.

A Coach purse for $1,000.

An Armani suit for $2,000.

There are low-cost alternatives to all of the above, but each year thousands of people write the big checks because the value is perceived to warrant the price.

Remember, when it comes to product pricing, perceived value will win out over logical value every time.

CHAPTER 23

What's in a Name?
When It Comes to
Your Business, Plenty

What's harder to name: a new baby or a new business? Coming from parents with the names Claude and Gertrude, you'd probably expect me to say that naming a new baby is harder, but you'd be wrong. Even if you name a child something totally silly like Apple or Moon Unit or Butterscotch or Bubba you're probably not dooming it to failure. Ridicule, yes, bullying, definitely, but failure, probably not.

Deciding on a business name, however, is one of the most important decisions you will ever make as an entrepreneur. The right business name can help you rise above the crowd, while the wrong business name can leave you trampled in the rush.

With the economy in a slump and competition on the rise, now more than ever it is important that you put considerable thought into coming up with the perfect name for your business.

No one would deposit their money in "Fred's Bank" or drop off their dry cleaning at "We Suck Less Than the Other Guys Martinizing."

Unfortunately, finding the perfect business name is a task that is easier said than done. It seems like all the good business names are either married or gay. No wait, that's a different subject, but the analogy holds true.

We live in an age when a business called "The Body Shop" might repair wrecked cars or sell skintight jeans to teenagers, so before you send your letterhead to the printer, consider the following points to help you select the business name that's right for you.

The first thing you should do is conduct a little research to determine if the name is already in use by someone else. You would be surprised at how many entrepreneurs forget to research this point and open a business with a name that is already in use by someone else.

Check with the county clerk and the secretary of state to make sure the name isn't already licensed for use or incorporated with the state. Also check with the U.S. Patent and Trademark office to see if the name is already trademarked by someone else. Using another company's trademark exposes you to legal action by the trademark owner. Even if your name is just similar to the trademarked name, you may find yourself in court defending your right to use the name. And odds are it's a battle you will lose.

If the name you choose is not in use, you should immediately reserve the name with the secretary of state (if you plan on incorporating) and apply for a trademark to ensure your legal ownership. If you do not trademark the name someone can come along later and attempt to steal the name out from under you. Imagine spending years building up your business only to have some upstart trademark the name and engage you in a legal battle over rightful ownership. This is one fight you don't need, especially when the hassle could have been easily avoided with a few bucks and a few forms.

Another important thing to consider is the domain name for your business. The domain name is the website address a customer will use to find you on the Web. Is the domain name for your business name available? If not, is there a domain similar to the business name you're considering?

You will undoubtedly discover that securing a suitable domain name is actually harder than choosing a business name. Most logical domain names are already reserved, but you might get lucky. Keep in mind that domain names should be short and descriptive, and preferably have the .com or .net extension. You can use other extensions (I've even used the ".to" extension on occasion) if necessary; just keep in mind that you will need to put forth a little extra marketing effort to promote the website address as people typically assume a .com extension as the norm. Whatever you do, don't use a domain name that is a confusing amalgam of letters and numbers that is hard to remember and even harder for your customer to type in.

One good way to approach the task of naming a business is to do so from your customer's point of view. Your business name should clearly define your offering and communicate your message to customers. Put yourself in your customer's shoes for a moment. If you were looking for a business that provides your product or service, what would you expect that business to be called? If you were in the market for computer parts, for example, wouldn't you look for a business that has "computer parts" reflected in the business name? Jim's Computer Parts may not sound as snazzy as Jim's Electronics Emporium, but snazzy doesn't pay the bills. Happy customers who quickly identify you as the source of their purchase do.

The name of your business can also spark subconscious reactions in customers that may drive them to you or drive them away. Words like *quality*, *complete*, *executive*, *best*, *low-cost*, and *on-time* often spark positive reactions in the mind of the consumer. Words like *cheap*, *discount*, and *used* tend to create negative emotions. You'll notice that no one claims to sell used cars anymore, but the dealer lots are loaded with vehicles that are "previously owned."

Finally, let's talk about things to avoid. Experts agree that you should avoid using generic terms like *enterprise*, *corporation*, *partners*, and *unlimited* as part of your everyday business name. These terms are fine for the legal business entity name, but are often too unclear for everyday use. Can you tell me what any of these companies do: ABC Corporation, Big Dog Enterprises, M&B Partners, and Discounts Unlimited? I didn't think so, and neither can potential customers.

Also avoid abstract names like Yahoo! and Google. Abstract names will require a subtitle to explain what the business does or an expensive marketing campaign that brands the name into the minds of consumers. Unless you have deep pockets, I suggest you go with a name that describes your business at first glance and leave abstraction to the likes of Cher.

Finally, you should avoid hokey names, unless of course, you are starting a hokey business.

Crazy Dave's Stereo Shop is a great name if the business is really run by Crazy Dave and his personality is exploited in the marketing of the business. However, if you want to be taken seriously, then give your business a serious name.

Would you go to Crazy Dave's House of Dentistry?

Neither would I, brother.

Neither would I.

CHAPTER 24

When Signing a Lease, Look for the Words "First Born"

For entrepreneurs who have never rented commercial space before, moving into that first office or storefront is an exciting experience that serves to validate their membership in the Official Entrepreneur's Club and makes them feel that they have arrived (poor saps).

They are like little entrepreneurial debutantes at their first cotillion. They stage an elaborate ribbon-cutting ceremony that involves the mayor and a giant pair of scissors that would barely cut butter.

They invite the entire membership of the Chamber of Commerce, all their customers and vendors, total strangers they meet on the way to work, and all their friends and family. The more the merrier! There's a big cake with their logo on it and they hand out 25-cent pens that have their company name screened on the side, and a good time is had by all.

Then reality sets in and they awake to find that they used one of those 25-cent pens to affix their signature to an ironclad lease that is invariably slanted in favor of the landlord. By the time they use that pen to sign the next month's rent check, they often find themselves sitting in a leased space that does not suit their needs, staring at a

5-year lease that they really don't understand, wondering just what the hell they have gotten themselves into.

And their first-born child is nowhere to be found.

But you can't really blame them for being excited. Putting your name on a commercial lease is one of the first tangible commitments an entrepreneur makes to his or her business, and searching for that first office or retail space can be a truly invigorating experience.

We entrepreneurs like to imagine ourselves as modern-day explorers, going out into the cold, cruel, commercial world to plant the company flag in our own little piece of rented real estate. I remember that feeling of triumph when I rented my first office so many years ago.

It's funny how you never get the same feeling when laying claim to future office space. For us old timers, searching for new office space is about as exciting as watching paint dry on our old office wall.

Many entrepreneurs get so caught up in the spell of their first commercial space that they fail to look beyond their immediate needs. You can't predict the future, but the biggest mistake you can make when leasing space is to put very little thought into whether the space will suit your needs for the long term.

So my first advice to you is to curb your excitement and call in a professional to help you find the perfect space for your business. A good realtor or commercial leasing agent not only can save you time and money, but can also help you avoid mistakes that can cost you thousands of dollars over the course of your lease. They can help you locate property, negotiate with landlords, and possibly spot problems with the space or neighborhood that you might have missed.

My second bit of advice is this: Once you find a space that suits your needs, have an attorney look over the lease agreement before you sign it. A commercial lease is a legally binding agreement that should not be taken lightly. I have found that many entrepreneurs never even take time to read the lease until they try to get out of it, which is always too late and always impossible to do.

It's easier to break a bond with Satan than to get out of a commercial lease.

When you sign a lease on behalf of your business, you are the one on the hook for the remaining cost of the lease should your business decline and no longer have revenue to cover the rent. It's worth the money to pay an attorney to make sure that your interests are covered.

My third bit of advice is to imagine your needs down the road, not just in the here and now. Rarely will you find a landlord willing to grant a lease for less than one year. Most leases are three to five years in length, which means you must take future growth into consideration when looking for space. It wouldn't be wise to sign a 5-year lease on a 1,000-square-foot office if you think you might outgrow the space within a year or two. That's why it's a good idea to request a clause in the lease that gives you an out if your company outgrows the space.

Here are a few other points to consider when shopping for commercial space:

Location, location, location. If your business involves walk-in traffic, location is a huge factor to be considered. Is the location convenient to your customers? Is the neighborhood growing or going downhill? Are there major improvements or renovations taking place or are businesses moving out in droves? Is the property zoned for your kind of business?

Is there sufficient parking for customers and employees? Parking is especially important for a retail store, but also for any business that may have customers coming and going. Very few customers will park four blocks away and hike back to your door. A lack of parking can drive you out of business.

Also take into account the number of employees you have now and expect to have in the future. The number of bodies inhabiting the space will help dictate the amount of space needed. Employees get awful grumpy when stacked up like cordwood (trust me on this one). You should have enough space for everyone to work comfortably.

When leasing commercial space the devil is often in the (overlooked) details. If you will be using computers and lots of electronics, make sure the building's electrical system will support your needs. It's a terrible feeling to turn on your computer and blow every lightbulb in the place.

If you like a quiet work environment and your office windows are 20 feet from the street, you'll be in for a rude awakening when the rush-hour traffic hits.

If the air conditioning in your office is controlled by the thermostat in a neighboring suite that is inhabited by an old lady who freezes in 90-degree weather, you will be in for a very long, very hot summer.

One of the biggest mistakes you can make as an entrepreneur and lessee of commercial space is not having an attorney review the lease. And forget reading the fine print. When it comes to a commercial lease, it's *all* fine print.

Don't believe me? Let me tell you the true story of my friend Homer, whose name I have changed to protect the ignorant. Homer signed a two-year lease on a suite of offices for his business. As the owner of the business, Homer signed on the dotted line and agreed to personally guarantee payment of the lease and to abide by its terms. Homer moved in and it was business as usual until the end of the two-year lease term drew near. It was then that Homer discovered that failing to read the lease was about to bite him in the butt.

Toward the end of the two-year lease period Homer decided to relocate, but when he gave the landlord what he thought was the customary 30-day notice, he discovered that the lease had automatically renewed for another two-year term at the 60-day notice point. In other words, Homer didn't realize that the lease required a minimum of 60 days' notice to let the landlord know that the lease would not be renewed.

Because Homer did not know that he was required to give at least 60 days' notice of his intent to vacate, the lease automatically renewed for another two years. And there was not a darn thing Homer could do about it but back himself into an ass-kicking machine for not taking the time to read the lease or having an attorney review it.

What was the landlord's position when Homer pointed out that he had not read the lease and therefore was not aware of the 60-day notice? The landlord, while sympathetic to Homer's plight, stuck to his guns and told Homer that he would have to honor the lease, which meant that even if Homer moved out as planned, he was still on the hook for paying the rent for another two years.

Does the fact that the landlord chose to enforce the lease agreement rather than let Homer off the hook make him an evil man? Not at all. From the landlord's point of view, he had no choice but to enforce the terms of the lease. He had a signed contract that told him his space was going to be rented for the next two years. He had not planned on the space suddenly being vacant. Being a landlord with vacant space is like being a business with no paying customers. Empty space means no revenue from rental fees, which means no money to pay the mortgage payment. As the old saying goes, "No offense, it's just business."

Sure, any landlord with a heart might feel bad that Homer was ignorant of the auto-renewal clause, but not so bad that he is willing to risk his own financial well-being by having Homer's space sit vacant. The bottom line is this: Whether Homer read the lease or not is irrelevant. Homer signed the lease, thereby agreeing to its terms, and therefore he must hold up his end of the bargain, period.

Homer went ahead and relocated his business in spite of not being able to get out of his old lease, and he continued paying the payment on the vacated space until he was able to sublet it many months later. Thousands of dollars were flushed down the drain because Homer didn't take the time to do things right on the front end. I can assure you it is a mistake he will never make again.

The moral to this story is *read the lease*. Or even better, have an attorney read it for you. I have learned over the years to never sign a legal document of any kind without letting my attorney review it, especially if the document involves money and my first-born child.

Here are a few other points to ponder before signing a commercial lease.

How is the lease payment calculated? The most basic equation for calculating a lease payment takes the number of square feet times the cost per square foot, then amortizes that over a 12-month span. For example, if you have 1,000 square feet and the cost per square foot is $12, the annual lease payment would be $12,000. Divided by

12 months, the monthly lease payment would be $1,000. Again, this is a simplified scenario. These days most commercial leases include additional factors that affect the final price, such as rent increases, operating expense escalations, common area charges, and so forth.

Who pays for what? It's important that you understand exactly what you are paying for. Are you responsible for any costs other than the rent? Will you be responsible for paying your own utilities, for example? Will you have to pay for parking privileges or janitorial service? Who handles maintenance and repairs?

Is there an escalation clause? It is typical that the lease contain what's known as an escalation clause that allows the landlord to pass on increased building operating expenses to the tenants. If your lease contains such a clause, you should ask for a cap on the amount the lease payment may rise over a given period of time. And if the escalation clause is ever activated by the landlord, you are well within your rights to ask for an itemized accounting of the expenses that are being considered as cause for your raise in rent.

What rent increases might there be? One very important factor to know is this: If you do renew the lease, how much can the landlord go up on the rent? It is expected that rents will increase as property values increase. If your landlord can rent the space for more than you agreed to pay a year ago, he is within his rights to ask for the increase. However, it would be a nightmare if your rent suddenly doubled overnight. Negotiate the increase before you sign the lease. Most rent increases are calculated by percentage, not by flat rates.

Renewals and terminations. Most leases require that you give a minimum of 60 days' notice if you intend to terminate the lease and vacate the property. As Homer learned, many leases also renew automatically for another term unless you give notice within 60 days of expiration. Know when your lease expires and the time required to give notice.

Is a personal guarantee required? What happens if your business goes south and you can no longer afford to make the lease payment? Are you then responsible for paying the rent out of your own pocket? Probably so. Most landlords insist on a personal guarantee from the owner or an officer of the business. This means that even if you go out of business you are still personally on the hook for the remainder of the lease.

Finally, clarify all points. You should be clear on every point in the lease. And if you are not, ask for clarification. Exactly what space are you leasing? Who is responsible for repairs? What common areas will you have access to? Who is responsible for maintaining the little things, like keeping the shared restrooms stocked with soap, towels, and most importantly, toilet paper?

A small detail to consider now, but not when you suddenly find yourself without such amenities at the wrong time.

CHAPTER 25

Never Borrow Money from Anyone Who Sits Across from You at Thanksgiving Dinner

S ometimes being a business advice columnist is a little like be-ing Dear Abby. The questions may pertain to business, but the advice they are seeking is more of a personal nature. For inspiration during those Dear Abby times I like to don a great big old wig I bought at the Salvation Army that looks like something bees would nest in and a nice pink pants suit and dress sandals. I know that may be way more information than you need to know, but I think it's important that you understand the lengths I go to for my readers.

Plus I look stunning in pink.

Sometimes the questions don't come from entrepreneurs, but from their family and friends who are concerned that their loved one might be biting off more than he can chew. And sometimes that bite is coming out of Mom and Dad's bank account.

Case in point: One of my entrepreneurial students brought his dad along to one of the classes and during a break Dad pulled me aside and said something to the effect of the following.

"My son wants to borrow $5,000 to start this business he's been talking about. My wife is afraid to tell him no. She thinks we should just give him the money and not expect anything in return."

"Well, what do you think?" I asked.

He frowned and lowered his voice. "I don't think just giving him the money will teach him anything about business or responsibility. He doesn't have a very good track record with paying back borrowed money, so I'm a little worried that my investment will be lost. Should I loan him the money and hope for the best or just tell him no and hope he doesn't get too upset?"

Dang, how did I end up in the middle of this family feud? And I'm not even wearing my lucky Dear Abby wig! I told him to let me think about his situation and e-mail him the next day.

I knew how dear old Dad felt. There have been times when I've felt like my family's personal ATM machine. I don't mean this bad, but friends and relatives will take advantage of your good fortune and your good nature and your good will faster and more often than strangers will, as this gentleman obviously knew from past experiences with his son.

If you've ever been hit up for money by a friend or relative for anything, business or otherwise, and were never paid back, join the club and take the following advice to heart. And if you've ever hit up a friend or relative for money and never paid it back, shame on you. And if you're an entrepreneur looking to raise money for your venture from friends or family, pay close attention.

Here's the e-mail that I sent him the next day.

Mr. Rogers, the first thing you need to do is determine if this money would be offered to your son in the form of a gift, loan, or investment. Our conversation tells me that you have not yet made that all-important distinction.

It sounds like your wife wants to make a gift of the money, expecting nothing in return but the undying love of her last-born son.

You, on the other hand, don't know if you should offer the money as a loan (*Should I loan him the money*) or as an investment (*I'm worried that my investment will be lost*).

Until you can make that distinction, your money should remain in the bank.

I have a very simple rule when it comes to loaning money to relatives: *Never, never, never, never, ever* loan money to anyone you might have to sit next to at Thanksgiving dinner. Do you need me to repeat that or are we good?

"Son, pass me that dressing and tell everybody the story of how you blew your old mom and dad's retirement money on that silly business idea of yours."

A loan from a relative is no different from a loan from a bank. You, Mr. Banker, are giving your son, Mr. Borrower, the use of your money for a specific period of time and you fully expect the loan to be paid back under specific terms, even if his business goes south. Sure, you will probably be a little more forgiving than a bank when the loan goes unpaid, but the damage to your personal relationship could be extreme and hard to repair.

In the most basic of terms, if you loan your son the money you become the creditor and he becomes the debtor. Have you ever heard of a creditor and debtor having a very good relationship? Has Visa ever called you up just to ask how you're doing? Has your mortgage company ever named a kid after you? Has Finance America ever called to ask why you don't call your mother anymore? Probably not.

The same rule applies to investing in a relative's business. I have raised money for several business ventures and not once did I ever think about asking my relatives to chip in. The last thing I'd ever want to do is lose my mother's yardsale money. I'd never hear the end of it!

An investment is made with the understanding that your money is totally at risk with no guarantee of return. Even under the best of conditions an investment in any business is a gamble. You are betting your money that the business will be successful and that you will get a payback at some point in the future.

Hug your money real tight before making the investment because if the business doesn't make it, you will never see your money again.

You and your wife also seem very worried about making your son mad, which raises another huge red flag for me. If your son isn't mature enough to take the word "no" without getting upset, he's certainly not mature enough to start and run a business, unless that business is a bicycle paper route, and even then I wouldn't put my money on his chances of success.

The bottom line is this: If you can afford to give your son the money and can do so without attaching strings to it, then by all means give him the money and wish him well. Encourage his entrepreneurial spirit and support him as a parent should.

Do not, however, expect anything in return and never bring up the money again, especially if he's the one carving the turkey on Thanksgiving Day.

CHAPTER 26

Operator Error Is Why Most Businesses Really Fail

No book on business startup would be complete without addressing the topic of why most businesses fail within the first few years. You've seen the statistics so I won't regurgitate them here. Suffice it to say that a majority of startups fail within the first few years for a variety of reasons and with a variety of excuses.

"The market was just too tough."

"I ran out of money."

"I had no idea costs were going to be that high."

"Nobody would buy my product."

"The competition killed us."

"My partner cleaned out the bank account and ran off with his secretary."

Such excuses, most of which are common among reasons given for business failure, bring up a more important question and that is this: Do businesses fail or does the entrepreneur in charge of them fail?

It's not a popular opinion, but I think most business failures should be laid at the feet of the person in charge, not blamed on stiff competition, a lack of customers, down markets, or partners with low morals.

Sure, there may be contributing factors to the demise of a business, such as a huge chain store moving in next door, a down economy, the lack of qualified employees, new government regulations, the failure of a strategic partner, and so forth, but any entrepreneur worth his salt should see such things coming and make adjustments to weather the storm.

And the truth is sometimes the storm can't be weathered and you have to abandon ship. Is that a business failure or an entrepreneurial failure? I think the coin flips both ways.

Starting a business is never easy, and if you need stats to substantiate that fact here they are. Approximately half of all small businesses fail within the first four years, with a large percentage of those failures occurring in year one, and it's my opinion that most of those failures can be traced back to mistakes made by the human being or beings in charge.

You see, business itself is not inherently risky. Most business concepts have been proven to work with proper execution, funding, and management. It is when the human factor fails that the business suffers.

And I'm not just talking to hear my head rattle. According to a 2003 survey by U.S. Bank, the majority of business failures can be attributed to three reasons: bad management, bad financial planning, and bad marketing. Again, all are areas with a human theme in common.

The survey showed that 78 percent of the business failures examined were due in part to the lack of a well-developed business plan and a business owner who had no business being in the business he was in.

In other words, the business owner did not have adequate knowledge or a thorough understanding of the business he had chosen to start. This is why software entrepreneurs like me don't start shoe stores. I have feet, I wear shoes, but that's not enough to qualify me to go into the shoe business.

Seventy-three percent of the businesses surveyed were also managed by owners with rose-colored calculators. These optimistic entrepreneurs overestimated revenue and underestimated cost.

Seventy percent of the failed businesses were led by entrepreneurs who were in denial regarding their own competence, or more to the point, their own incompetence. These business owners either didn't recognize (or more likely chose to ignore) their own entrepreneurial shortcomings. These entrepreneurs also did not seek assistance from others who might have made up for their inadequacies. It's hard to ask for help when you are supposed to be the one with all the answers. It's harder still to lose your life savings when your business tanks.

The final contributing factor to the death of 63 percent of the businesses that died from bad management was that the owners had no relevant or applicable business experience. Just because you eat at McDonald's does not mean you're qualified to manage one.

Bad financial planning was the second reason why most businesses fail. According to the study, 82 percent of the business failures studied reported poor cash flow management as a contributing factor to the death of the business.

Seventy-nine percent of the businesses were inadequately funded to begin with and 77 percent miscalculated the cost of doing business. In other words, they failed to take into account all of the costs involved when setting the price for their products.

Bad marketing was a contributing factor in the death of 64 percent of the businesses surveyed. Many of these misguided entrepreneurs either minimized the importance of marketing and promotion or ignored it totally.

A vital part of marketing is knowing who your competition is and always knowing what they are up to. The entrepreneur who ignores his competition is a fool (gee, was that too harsh?) and is always destined to fail, as proven by the owners of the 55 percent of the dead businesses in the survey who either didn't even know who their competition was or simply chose to ignore the competition altogether.

Here's a nice hole in the sand for you, sir. Please insert your head.

Another mistake made by 47 percent of the deceased businesses was that they relied on just one or two customers for the bulk of revenues.

This is a common mistake made by many business owners who devote all their energy to one huge client. What they don't seem to understand is that if the one customer goes away, so does most of their revenue.

So what can you do to help ensure that your business doesn't end up as a statistic in some dumb old business failure survey? Read on and pay attention, my human friend.

Always have a plan. Many businesses fail because the owner failed to plan, or more to the point, failed to have a plan. Confucius say, "He who runs a business by the seat of his pants often ends up flat on his you-know-what." Okay, I made that up, but I bet Confucius thought of it at some point.

The problem is we entrepreneurs hate having to write business plans. Show me an entrepreneur who loves to write business plans and I'll show you a guy with too much time on his hands.

Look, Bubba, I know business plans are a pain to write and are often out of date the moment you finish them, but you must have a comprehensive business plan that roadmaps where you want your business to go and details how it will get there.

A good business plan will help you keep a handle on things like financials (income and outgo), sales and marketing, growth and burn rates, and a wide assortment of other factors. If it affects your business, it should be in your business plan.

Get rid of your rose-colored glasses. Always overestimate the amount of money that you will need to start the business and the amount it will take to sustain the business through the first year or two, or until the revenues can fully sustain the business. This is the number-one mistake made by entrepreneurs and the number-one reason businesses fail. If you think you'll need $100,000 to get you to stability, count on actually needing $200,000 or more.

Always pinch every penny until it screams. In business, money seems to evaporate at the touch, so it's vital that you manage your money wisely. If you don't know what your money's doing, odds are it's not doing what you think it is. Hire a good accountant and let him do his job. Review your financials with him at least once per quarter (if not monthly) and ask for reports you can review.

Always have experience in the type of business you're starting. And always have a thorough understanding of the industry. Many entrepreneurs start businesses that they have no business starting. This is like trying to fly a plane with no prior piloting experience. Always work in a business similar to the one you want to start before striking out on your own. We covered this already in an earlier chapter.

Never try to be all things to your business. It is unrealistic to think that you can perform every function in your business and still have time to build the business. You should perform only those tasks that you do well and help make the business stronger. Everything else you should either turn over to an employee or farm out to someone else.

Remember the old axiom, "Work on your business, not in it!"

Always keep an eye on the competition. If someone asks who your competition is and you can't immediately come up with at least two or three names, your business is in trouble. Every business has competition. A lack of competition means that there is probably no market for your product. Always know who your competition is and what they are doing or you might wake up one day to find that they have put you out of business.

Always know who your customers are and always strive to find new ways to serve them. Many small businesses don't really know who their customers are or what they can do to make the customer's experience with them better. A happy customer is a repeat customer who refers new customers. A current customer is worth far more than a potential customer. It's vital that you know who your customers are and understand why they do business with you. Once you have a customer, work hard to keep him and never stop trying to impress him. Customer service should be at the forefront of your business plan.

Always hire the best people you can find. Your employees are often the first line of contact your business has with the public. That's why the team you assemble to work in your business can make or break you. Don't hire anyone who does not impress you as a person. Train your employees well. They should know your business as well as you do. In the customer's eyes your employees are a direct reflection on you. Remember that when interviewing and hiring someone to interact with your customers.

Never put off till tomorrow what you can get done today. Procrastination is a bad thing when it comes to running a business. When the pile on your desk gets so high you can't see over it, it's time to get out from behind the desk and go to work. If you need help, take a time management class or hire an assistant. Otherwise you'll end up hiding behind that pile of papers when the collectors come to take your desk away.

Never be afraid to ask for help. No man (or woman) is an island. And no entrepreneur knows everything, even though we think we do. Put your pride in a drawer. If you need help, ask for it! That's why God made consultants.

Never undertake a task you have no experience or talent to perform. If you have no business doing the books, hire an accountant. If you need legal assistance, hire an attorney. If you can't draw a straight line, don't design your company logo.

Always be flexible. Times change, so must your business. Don't be so rigid that you can't adapt to new technologies or new customer demands. Many businesses are totally retooled every few years. Yours might be one of them.

Always keeping learning. Be a sponge. Read every business book you can get your hands on. Attend seminars and lectures. Never stop learning. Contrary to what you believe, there is still plenty of open space in your head. Fill it with knowledge that you can use to make your business a success.

CHAPTER 27

Do a CSI on a Failed Business to Discover the Real Cause of Death

Even with all my sage advice in the previous chapter, businesses will still continue to fail at a rate of thousands every year. Sometimes you do everything you can possibly do, you make all the right decisions and all the right moves, and still the business goes belly up.

So what? That's how it works. It happens to the best of us. Just about every entrepreneur I know has a failed business or two under his belt, including me. We entrepreneurs are risk takers, we put ourselves out there, we go where others fear to tread, we take our chances and give it our best shot; and sometimes we miss. The key is learning from failure, not wallowing in it like a mud hole.

Case in point: Consider the following question from Gene, who was in the throes of a business that was about to go under for the last time.

Q: Tim, after years of dreaming about starting my own business, I finally took the plunge a little over a year ago. To say the least, my dream quickly became a nightmare. The business didn't do nearly as well as I had hoped. I ran out of money within six months and had to take out a second mortgage on my house just to keep things going. I have now closed the business and am left with a pile of bills that will probably put me in personal bankruptcy. I don't mean to take it out on you, but instead of telling people how great having your own business is all the time you should also warn them that starting a business is not easy and can be devastating when things go wrong.

A: Gene, I hope that I have never given anyone the impression that having your own business is a walk in the park. To the contrary, I'm like Chicken Little when it comes to warning readers of the obstacles and pitfalls that await those considering the entrepreneurial plunge.

Just to make sure we're in agreement, let me reiterate the standard warnings once again. Starting a business is incredibly hard work. It takes long hours and deep pockets. It demands unbridled passion and unquestioned commitment. It requires that you give of yourself until you often feel there is nothing left to give.

And sometimes, even after you've done all that you can do and given all that you can give, the business fails. Period.

Blood, sweat, and tears can carry you only so far in the business world. Good intentions and grand ideas won't pay the office rent. You cannot make payroll with Monopoly money. Believe me, I've tried. It's my fault for hiring smart employees . . .

I certainly don't mean to make light of your situation. In fact, I know exactly how you feel. I failed so miserably my first time in business that I swore I would never think about working for myself again.

All I wanted to do was to find a nice, secure 9-to-5 job that I could crawl back to that provided me with a nice steady paycheck. I yearned for the opportunity to grow fat and happy on someone else's payroll for a change.

I never again wanted to have to think about customers or vendors or employees or withholding taxes or accounts receivable or anything else even remotely associated with being in business.

I just wanted to crawl in a hole and die because my business had failed, and in my All-American, macho male, "you are what you do" brain that meant I was a failure, too.

Getting over the failure of a business can be extremely difficult, especially if you are one of those entrepreneurs (like I was) who relates the success or failure of a business to the success or failure of you as a person.

The best way that I know of to get over the failure of a business (and the deep feelings of personal failure that go along with it) is to do an autopsy of the business to help find out exactly what went wrong.

Only by discovering our weakness can we build on our strengths (Yogi Berra, eat your heart out).

It took a long time and an enormous amount of reflection to realize that the business had failed for many reasons, not simply because I was a miserable excuse for an entrepreneur. I wasn't looking to shuck the blame so much as simply trying to understand what really went wrong.

A few years later when I mustered the courage to take the plunge again, I did so with the knowledge gained from my first failed business. I knew what I had done wrong and I knew what I'd done right. Lessons learned, put to good use. Knock wood, this time so far, so good.

Performing an autopsy on a failed business is a simple process, but one that can reveal a wealth of information that you can use should you ever decide to step out onto the business high wire again.

To do your business autopsy, find a quiet place where you can sit and reflect on the life of your business. With pen and paper in hand (or laptop on lap) write down everything that you can think of that went right with the business and, alternatively, everything that went wrong. Your goal is to create a "Success" versus "Failure" spreadsheet that will help you better understand exactly why the business went south.

For the autopsy to be effective, it is imperative that you are completely honest with yourself. Shove your ego in a box and be completely realistic or the autopsy will just become an exercise in futility. You will end up looking for scapegoats instead of reasons.

If your lack of experience was a contributing factor to the failure of the business, write it down.

If your brilliant negotiating skills allowed you to close a big deal and beat out a competitor, write it down.

If you were undercapitalized or incorrectly estimated your share of the market, write it down.

If you had a partner who didn't pull his weight or a product that didn't sell as well as you thought it would or your building was flattened by an earthquake, write it down. Write it all down.

Once you have all the facts in front of you, it's easy to see why the business really failed. You might be surprised to find out that the failure of the business wasn't completely your fault, after all.

Then again, you might discover that the business failure was your fault, just as you suspected. If that turns out to be the case, don't beat yourself up for long. We all make mistakes. We all screw up. That's life. The key is to learn from your mistakes so you don't make the same mistake again.

Not everyone is cut out to be an entrepreneur and that's okay.

The world would be a miserable place if everyone sat around whining about their lack of customers or complaining about their employees.

Moral to the story: Before diving in you should know the industry, know the market, and know the competition.

Leave your ego at home and ask for help when you need it.

Understand the importance of marketing and go out of your way to tell every person on the planet about your product.

And the biggie: Be realistic with the finances. Don't overestimate revenue and underestimate cost. Always estimate revenue on the low side and cost on the high side. If you blow those estimates out of the water by doubling your revenue numbers, good for you. You now have something to brag about rather than to cry over.

Will that guarantee the success of your business?

Not at all, but it sure can't hurt.

CHAPTER 28

Use Roadmapping to Plot Business and Personal Growth

When I was a kid my family often participated in that grand old American tradition called the Sunday drive. You remember those long, boring Sunday drives in the car with your family to nowhere?

Sure, it was better than sitting at home because we had only three TV channels to watch and cartoons were shown for only a few hours on Saturday morning, but when you got back home didn't you always feel that you hadn't really gone anywhere?

Technically, if you leave your house and don't stop until you reach your house, that's a round trip, not a fun outing.

I always hated those Sunday drives. And do you want to know what my kids would say if I asked, "Hey kids, who wants to take a long Sunday drive with Dad?" They'd tell me to take a pill and lie down.

More often than not we entrepreneurs are like those old Sunday drivers, only we travel at a much faster pace. We're barreling down the business highway at 90 miles an hour (twice the speed of the average Sunday drive) and we pray that something doesn't get in our way to slow us down or bring us to a crashing halt.

I've left a ton of entrepreneurial roadkill in my wake and I'm sure you have, too.

Who has time to worry about what's ahead when you're busy worrying about the here and now?

Most entrepreneurs don't have the time to look past lunch. They operate one hour at a time. They have no long-range plan that takes them past the next payroll. And the most important point of all is this: They are reactive rather than proactive. They let circumstances rule their efforts rather than anticipating and managing the circumstances as they come. Such short-sightedness has led many entrepreneurs to crash and burn.

For years I was a reactive entrepreneur, meaning that I reacted to circumstances rather than planned for them.

Now I am proactive. Instead of letting destiny determine the direction of my business, I am now in control. I now know exactly where I want my business to be in one year, two years, three years, and beyond.

I call the process "roadmapping" and here's how it works.

Determine your destination. Steven Covey said, "Start with the end in mind." Therefore the first step is to determine where you want to be in one year (or two or three), both personally and professionally. Don't forget that we entrepreneurs often blur the line between our personal and business lives, so you must take your personal desires into consideration along with your business goals.

If your destination is to have a business with a hundred employees and a million dollars in revenue, write that down. If your destination is to completely shift directions and start something new, write that down. Be as bold and outrageous as you want. Shoot for the moon rather than the horizon. Big endings start with big dreams. No matter how grandiose your plan, be as descriptive as you can. If your mind can envision it, your heart can make it happen.

Envision your destination. If you are planning a trip to the beach you can close your eyes and smell the ocean, hear the birds, feel the sand beneath your feet. You must be able to envision your destination with the same realism. Close your eyes and imagine your business in one year. Are you in the same location or in a new building? As you enter is there a lobby with a receptionist? Is she happy to see you? (Hopefully you don't envision her being unhappy to see you.) What about your employees? Are they happy and productive? Imagine every detail and write it down.

Determine your starting point. Now take an honest look at where your business is today. Close your eyes and imagine yourself walking into your business for the first time. What do you see and how does it differ from the business you just envisioned? What steps must you take to get from point A, where you are today, to point B, where you want your business to be in one, three, or five years?

Create your roadmap. The next step is to create the roadmap that will get you from point A to point B. Just as you wouldn't take a long road trip without a map or directions (unless you're a guy), you shouldn't plan a journey in business growth without a plan. Your roadmap will detail steps you must take to get you to your final destination. For example, if you envision dominating a certain market, what steps must you take to accomplish that goal? Perhaps making contacts in that market, doing market research, changing your business model, or coming up with a new product. All of these things should be listed on your roadmap.

Anticipate roadblocks. Finally, list what you see as the greatest challenges in the road ahead. Will you need funding for your adventure? Will you need to hire more employees? Are there competitors in your way? Are there impending market conditions that may prove hazardous? Identifying the roadblocks before you start your journey will help you prepare to deal with them when they pop up.

Hit the road today! Once you have your roadmap on paper you must get started right away or you're in danger of running out of gas. What actions can you take today, tomorrow, next week, next month, to get you where you want to be? Just having the plan does you absolutely no good. It's like having the keys to a sports car you never drive. You must concentrate on the plan every second of your day. You must do things that move you closer and closer to your destination. There should not be a single day that goes by when you are not moving ahead.

Repeat the process. When you reach the end of the road you are not finished. Each ending is a new beginning.

You plot a new destination, create a new roadmap, and keep going. Your business should be headed toward a destination every day, not just on a perpetual Sunday drive.

CHAPTER 29

Business Lessons Learned at the Mall

I recently took my teenage daughter shopping at the mall. The experience raised two questions. (1) What business lessons might be learned from such a foray into teen commerce; and (2) What the heck was I thinking?

Only the good Lord knows. I vaguely recall complaining to my wife that my 18-year-old daughter, Chelsea, didn't spend enough time with her dear old dad anymore.

It's a complaint that every dad of a teenage girl formerly known as "my baby" has made at one time or another. I also recall my insightful wife telling me that if I wanted to spend time with Chelsea now that she was a teenager I would have to do it in her element, which happens to be any large structure with the word "Mall" on the side.

A fitting analogy would be that if you want to spend time with a moody tiger you have to go into the jungle to do it.

No offense to my mall merchant brothers and sisters, but a trip naked into the deepest jungles of the Amazon is more appealing to me than a fully clothed trip to the mall. I get no joy out of trudging from store to store, attempting to communicate with salespeople from other planets, browsing discount racks of last season's dollar merchandise, and peering into windows at mannequins that seem to be in some sort of inanimate pain. Which brings up another question: Why can't they make a happy mannequin? I mean all they have to do is stand around in expensive clothes all day. What the heck do they have to be so unhappy about?

I guess it's a guy thing. It is programmed deep within my genetic code to hold such things as going to the mall and hanging out in the ladies undergarments section and holding her purse while my wife shops for panties (or drawers, as we call them in the south) in high disregard. But so strong is my love for my daughter that I pushed my true feelings aside and off we went to the mall on a rainy Saturday morning.

I called it, "Driving the green mile."

I was perfectly fine walking through Sears (a real man's store). I held my own when we cruised through Spencer's Gifts (I found the Ozzy Osborne bobble-head doll to be quite life-like), but when we walked into one of those stores that specialize in clothing and accessories for the younger generation, my psyche all but shut down.

Within minutes I found myself standing at the back of the store holding my daughter's purse while she tried on small swatches of material that the store was trying to pass off as clothing. Didn't I just say that I hated this kind of thing? Yet so strong was my love for my little girl that I willingly stood there clutching her purse while trying to look inconspicuous standing between the designer thongs and fancy padded bras, silently thanking God that I was a man and had no need for such uncomfortable-looking things. I suddenly understood why mannequins look so unhappy.

So let's get back to my first question: Are there business lessons that can be learned from a trip to the mall?

As the young folks would say, "Dude, definitely!"

The following observations, while being made from a vantage point that most men would never admit to, can be applied to every business, not just to retailers that cater to Generation Why.

Know thy customer well. Not just from a demographic standpoint, but up close and personal. Even from my limited vantage point behind the rack of neon tube tops it was easy to identify the store's typical customer: young, hip females, ages mid-teens to mid-twenties.

They wandered through in groups of twos and threes. I suppose that going to the restroom in public and shopping are the two things females must do in groups. It makes perfect sense when you realize that for teenage girls (and many grown women, I'm told) shopping is a social activity, an excursion to be taken with friends. The smart retailers know this and design their stores to be as much a social hot spot as a retail establishment.

From the hip/cool music blaring from the overhead speakers to the hip/cool young sales dudes to the hip/cool posters on the walls to the hip/cool selection of merchandise, this store was a teenage girl's retail heaven on earth. And the constantly ringing cash register proved that they were doing something right.

Target your product to a growing customer base. Teens represent one of the fastest-growing segments of the consumer population, registering a growth of 16.6 percent between 1990 and 2000. Teens also wield significant buying power, both in their own right and in the context of their family purchasing decisions.

Recent studies have shown that teenagers age 15 to 19 spend as much as $100 per week, much of it on clothing and accessories. That's why this expanding segment of the buying public is increasingly being targeted by smart marketers like Old Navy, The Gap, The Buckle, Pac Sun, and many others.

As the old business saw goes, "Sniff for money, then follow your nose."

Provide great customer service. I've preached this sermon before. Know what your customers expect and always overdeliver. Cater to their whims. Ask their name and use it with respect. Make them feel like your friend, not your meal ticket. Make their experience a good one and they will return. This store knew the value of great customer service. Every employee was upbeat and helpful; even the one who asked if I needed a chair did so with a smile. I guess it was obvious that my poor, tired old legs were about to give out. Still, if he had called me "Pops" I would have beaten him to death with my cane, smile or no smile.

Good employees make all the difference. Hire enthusiastic people and train them well. The manager of this store, who looked all of 16 but privately professed to be 26, was one of the best salesmen I have ever seen. He dressed like his customers. He spoke their language. He knew their likes and dislikes. He was well-versed on fashion trends. He pointed out things that might be of interest to them and immediately agreed with whatever their opinion was.

"You'd look great in this shirt," he told a giggling gaggle of girls. It didn't seem to matter that he wasn't speaking to any one of them in particular. They all giggled some more and trotted off to the fitting rooms to try on shirts. You could almost hear the cash register ring.

Upsell, Upsell, Upsell. Millions of dollars have been made by asking one simple question: "Do you want fries with that?" When it came time to check out the young manager went into upsell mode by saying things like, "That's a great shirt you're buying—we have a really cool pair of shorts to match that! These earrings are on sale. They would look awesome with that necklace you're wearing!"

My daughter giggled and blushed with each compliment-slash-sales pitch, and if I had not been the one holding the credit card, she would have bought everything he was selling.

During the ride home Chelsea made the defining comment of the day.

"What a great store!" she gushed. "I bet they sell a lot more stuff because of that cute sales guy!"

Business wisdom from the mouths of babes.

I should've had sons.

CHAPTER 30

Piercings, Tattoos, and Other Important Matters of Business

I've been expanding my entrepreneurial horizons lately by meeting entrepreneurs in businesses I'd never been exposed to before. I learned that there are many kinds of entrepreneurs and each dances to his own drummer.

Some do it the right way while others do it however they dang well please. I have found that their attitude determines the quality of work they do and most likely how long they will stay in business.

Case in point: My aforementioned teenage daughter, Chelsea, decided that the world would come to a screeching halt if she didn't get her belly button pierced. Yes, I said, "belly button pierced," which to me sounds about as sane as "having your head waxed and painted blue," but I'm told belly button piercing is all the rage, even with girls whose bellies should never be exposed under penalty of law (you know who you are, ladies).

Now I personally don't see the logic in having holes poked in your body other than those that the good Lord put there in the first place, but according to my daughter, "Daddy, all the girls are getting their belly buttons pierced."

To which I replied, "If all the girls were having their heads waxed and painted blue would you want to do that, too?"

To which she replied, "Dad, you're an idiot."

When she switches from "Daddy" to "Dad" I know I'm in trouble.

The conversation just went downhill from there and as usual I lost the argument when she used the magic words, "Mom said it was okay with her if it was okay with you."

Man, I hate it when the ball is bounced back into my court and I don't know how to hit it.

So I replied, "If your mom waxed her head and painted it blue . . ."

Now if I've learned anything in my life it is this: When I hear, "Mom says it's okay with her if it's okay with you," that either means it's really okay or it isn't really okay and she's putting the bad-guy hat on me and I'm supposed to put my foot down and say no. Since her mother wasn't around to give me hand signals, and calling her to verify the story would have meant that I didn't trust my sweet daughter (so I was told), I had to take her at her word. I gave my blessing to said piercing and wished her well.

Then the kicker came when she said, "And Mom said you should go with me to have it done."

Now I was with this child when she rode her first bike, when she put on her first pair of skates, when she danced her first dance with a boy, and when she bought her first brassiere (that's a whole other story), but I never thought I would have to hold her hand while she got a loop of surgical steel poked through her belly button. I wasn't sure I could watch such a thing without doing something violent to the person making my baby uncomfortable, but the duties of the modern father never end.

So off we go to a tattoo/piercing parlor. I have to be honest, I fully expected to walk into a place so dank and dirty that I would have grounds to kibosh this whole belly button piercing thing. To my surprise we walked into a facility that was well decorated and brightly lit, and probably more sterile and professionally run than most hospitals.

We were warmly greeted by a young fellow who was tattooed and pierced like a walking billboard to his industry. He had a thick hoop dangling from his nostrils, which I assume his wife used to hook a rope to and pull him around with, kind of like leading a brightly painted bull. First impressions go both ways: I'm sure he was wondering what this redneck wearing a Hawaiian shirt and torn jeans and cowboy boots was doing in his shop.

Then I realized he was a breed of entrepreneur (we can usually spot each other, like baboons can spot monkeys) and I immediately pulled out my microscope to inspect him and his business.

Tattoos and nose hoops aside, he was friendly, knowledgeable, professional, and supportive of his customer's needs. As I looked around the waiting area I could tell that his business was well-run and designed to make his customers feel confident and comfortable at the same time. There were large leather couches and lots of tattoo magazines and rock music blaring from the ceiling. Not exactly my element of choice, but it was perfectly suited for his target clientele.

The girl who actually did the piercing (an employee equally as friendly as the owner) was meticulous and thorough and seemed to be highly trained. And she took more time consulting with my daughter than any doctor has ever spent talking to me.

She made sure Chelsea and I understood the entire process and the ramifications. Only when she was convinced that Chelsea was positive in her decision and that I wasn't going to freak out did the piercing begin.

In the end, Chelsea got her belly button ring and I got my first exposure to an entrepreneur of another kind.

Maybe I'll get my belly button pierced.

I'd look good with one of those big old lion head knockers like you see on the doors at church hanging over my belt.

Anyway, all's well that ends well.

Then her mother called . . .

CHAPTER 31

How to Boost Your Bottom Line with Two Little Words

I hate to sound like one of those cheesy get-rich-quick commercials, but I am going to let you in on a little secret that is so powerful that it will immediately change the way you do business.

In fact, this little secret is so powerful that you will be amazed at its immediate effect on you, your employees, and your bottom line. This little secret is guaranteed to improve your relationship with current customers and if used wisely, can get you lots of new customers without spending a dime on marketing or advertising. It can endear them to your business and guarantee that they will be your customers for life.

The little secret is this: Whenever you have contact with your customers, whether it's in person, or by phone, fax, or e-mail, always use their name. That's it. The two little words that can drive your business through the roof are your customer's name.

When you use a customer's name the business experience suddenly becomes a personal one. And when the business experience becomes personal your customer becomes vested in the relationship and thereby becomes your friend. They become as concerned about your success as you are.

At the sound of his or her name your customer becomes your

champion. They will toot your horn and defend your honor. They will recommend you to their friends and be loyal to you to the end, even when they can get the same product or service elsewhere for less money.

Unfortunately, 99 percent of business owners and their employees fail to realize the importance of personalizing the business relationship. While they are happy to take my hard-earned dollars, most businesses could care less what my name is. That's why so many businesses fail: They see their customers as numbers, not names. The 1 percent of businesses that understand the impact of personalizing the business experience are the ones that will flourish.

Case in point: I'm the one at my office who goes through the mail every day, pulls out the checks, opens the envelopes, signs the checks, makes out the deposit slip, and takes the deposit to the bank. Sure, I could have someone else do this for me, but making the bank deposit is my absolute favorite thing about being an entrepreneur. Seeing numbers on a deposit slip validates my efforts. It is proof that I am doing something right, or at least my customers think I am.

So I go to the bank a lot. So much so that the young lady at the drive-through, whose name is Karen, knows me on sight and always seems genuinely happy to see me pull up.

"How are you today, Mr. Knox?" she always asks.

I can be in the lousiest mood of my life, but when I hear my name come through that speaker my mood immediately brightens. I always smile and chirp back: "I'm fine, Karen, how are you?" Okay, so I don't really chirp, but that's beside the point.

And it's even better if I have someone in the car with me. I have gone through that drive-through with business partners and customers in my car and when they hear "How are you today, Mr. Knox?" they are highly impressed, simply because Karen used my name.

"Wow," they always mutter. "They know you here, huh."

"Yep," I say proudly, ego adequately stroked. "I have all my accounts here: personal and business checking, savings, lines of credit, merchant account. This is the best dang bank on the planet. In fact, you should move all your accounts here."

And if my Mama is in the car with me and hears Karen use my name? Holy moly, she's one proud Mama! Okay, she's easily impressed, but again, that's beside the point.

Over the years I have probably recommended a dozen new customers to this bank, just because Karen, the wonderful drive-through teller who understands the value of good customer relations, uses my name every time I drive in.

Here's another example of how using a customer's name can add dollars to your bottom line. I was in Kansas City recently and stopped in at a Ruth's Chris Steakhouse for dinner. When I asked for a table the host asked for my name.

A few minutes later a young man came by to fill my water glass and asked, "Can I get you an iced tea, Mr. Knox?"

For a moment I thought I had a psychic waiter on my hands. Then it occurred to me that the host had obviously told the waiter my name and the waiter used it immediately to make me feel at home. Not as cool as having a psychic waiter, but pretty impressive nonetheless.

A few minutes later a different young man delivered bread to my table and said, "Here's your bread, Mr. Knox."

Before the night was over four different service people had visited my table and each used my name in a respectful manner. By the end of the meal I had spent $75 on dinner and dropped another $50 on tips.

Was it because the food was delicious? Yes, the food was excellent, but the truth is I felt like I had just had dinner with a bunch of friends. Granted, they were friends who were waiting hand and foot on me, but that just makes for better friends in my opinion.

It was an excellent dining experience, made even more so because they personalized the evening by using my name.

Do you think I now tell everyone I meet about this restaurant with the great food and the amazing service?

I'm telling you about it, aren't I?

CHAPTER 32

Most Customer Service People Are Walking Oxy-Morons

Nothing chaps my backside more than paying hard-earned money for a product or service only to have the provider of said product or service become apathetic, obnoxious, or just downright rude after the transactional smoke has cleared.

The bottom line, my entrepreneurial friend, is this: It doesn't matter if your product is fast food, slow food, retail goods, computers, lawnmowers, books, real estate, or automobiles, if a customer is willing to pay you good money in exchange for your product or service, that customer deserves to be treated with gratitude and respect, before, during, and after the sale. Period.

I'm constantly amazed at how many business owners and the frontline employees who represent them seem to forget this simple fact.

It's like the old saying about getting a little respect in the morning. If you court me before the sale, you damn well better respect me afterward. Just because you have my money in your pocket and I have your product in my hand that does not mean that my needs have been fully satisfied or that my expectations have ceased to exist. To the contrary, our relationship is just getting started. It's up to you how well we will get along and how long our relationship will last.

If the Almighty smote down every business that dispenses bad customer service the world would be a much friendlier, albeit much sparser place. Consider a world without malls and fast-food joints. Would it really be so bad?

Here's the point: Customer service should not stop after the sale. In fact, customer service *after* the sale can have greater impact on the success of your business than customer support before the sale.

Nothing generates negative buzz about a business like bad customer service, and nothing will drive nails in a business's coffin faster. News of bad customer service travels like lightning and spreads like wildfire.

Think back to the last time you were on the receiving end of bad customer service. I'd be willing to bet that you immediately went out into the world and told everyone you met about the experience. You probably also warned them to "never do business with those crooks or you'll get treated the same!"

As a businessperson, it should be your mission to make every customer a repeat customer, and one of the best ways to do that is by delivering superior customer service every time that customer comes through your door. Superior customer service leads to increased customer satisfaction, which leads to repeat business, which leads to customer loyalty. It is also much cheaper to keep a customer than to obtain a new one.

The fast-food industry is especially prone to customer service problems. This is due in large part to the fact that every transaction is a face-to-face sale and the average fast-food worker is a disgruntled teenager who would rather be lying on a bed of nails than standing behind a fast-food counter schlepping fries.

However, that doesn't always have to be the case. This is not meant as an ad for Chick-fil-A or as a slam at Taco Bell, but the difference in customer service between these two fast-food titans is astounding.

I used to frequent both establishments (fast food is my crack), so this is the voice of experience speaking. Behind the counter at the local Chick-fil-A are young people who seem genuinely happy to be of service. They are clean cut and polite. They don't wear their baseball caps sideways or have anything visibly pierced. They look me in the eye, they smile like there is no place on earth they would rather be, and they ask for my order in clear, concise English. They thank me profusely and invite me to come again. They provide excellent customer service before, during, and after the sale.

Conversely, a recent trip to a local Taco Bell almost ended on an episode of *Cops* because the young lady behind the counter grew angry when I politely pointed out that my nachos were stale and asked for a fresh bag (pet peeve #132: stale nachos). Miss Mary Sunshine snatched the offending nachos from my hand and slam dunked them in a trash can, then tossed a replacement bag (which were also stale) on the counter in front of me. She then gave me a look that clearly said that if I had any further complaints she'd be happy to escort me outside to discuss them in detail. I like nachos, but not so much that I would risk getting my butt kicked by a disgruntled teenage girl wearing a sideways Taco Bell cap.

This would be classified as not-so-excellent customer service before, during, and after the sale.

Now, which restaurant do you think I will go to the next time I feel the need to feed my fast-food monkey? And which restaurant do you think I enthusiastically recommend to my friends? The one that understands the importance of good customer service, of course.

The worst customer service experience I've ever had involved the purchase of a vehicle at a local used car lot. I purchased a used Ford Expedition on a Friday evening and when problems arose with the vehicle over the weekend, I went back to the dealership on Monday morning to speak with the sales manager. To say the least, the sales manager (who acted like my best friend on Friday) was not thrilled to see me on Monday. To make a very long story short, when I pointed out that he wasn't being very helpful after the sale he came around the desk yelling at the top of his lungs and waving his hands in my face. By the time the receptionist managed to calm him down, the sales manager had gone so far as to call me "a retarded idiot" (which may be considered redundant) and had instructed me to do something with the vehicle that I believe is anatomically impossible. It was an Expedition, I'm a little guy. Use your imagination.

Though the dealership owner later apologized and offered to take care of any problem I had, the damage to his business had already been done. The bad buzz machine started the second I left his lot.

Do you think I told everyone I met about my experience with that dealership? You bet your stale nachos I did. Do you think I will ever buy another car from that dealership? Not on your life. Do you think anyone I've told about the experience will buy a car from that dealership? Probably not. Do you think the owner and sales manager learned anything from the experience? We can only hope.

In the end, what is the value of great customer service?

Priceless, my friend, simply priceless.

Now, can somebody please get me some fresh nachos?

CHAPTER 33

You Should Never Stop Caring About What Your Customers Think

What truly puzzles me most is if bad customer service is such a death knell for business, why do so many businesses allow it to go on? I think the problem is that most bad customer service is doled out (or at least condoned) by business owners and managers who have ceased caring what their customers think. When you stop caring what your customers think it's time to close the doors. Go find a day job. You'll make someone a wonderfully disgruntled employee.

My latest parable of lousy customer service was actually experienced by my better half while attempting to buy my daughter a pair of basketball shoes. I won't mention the name of the sporting goods chain store in which the bad customer service took place, but I will tell you that its name is similar to the sound a frog with hiccups might make. Think Ribbett's.

As my wife waited for someone to assist her, the four or five teenagers who had been charged with manning the store stood in a clump at the cash register giggling and flirting with one another as if they were at the prom instead of at work.

When my wife pointed out this fact (she is not a shy woman), one of the employees, a cheeky lass of 16 or so, put her hands on her hips and said, "How rude!" The males in the group didn't react at all. They were too busy arguing over who could take a break so they could chase other cheeky lasses about the mall.

Needless to say my lovely bride, who has the ability to instill fear into the hearts of even the most worthless employees, left the gaggle of giggling teen idiots standing with their mouths open in disbelief. How dare a customer tell them to do that with a pair of basketball shoes?

Sadly, her experience was more common than not. Bigfoot sightings are more common than good customer service people these days. You have a better chance of finding Jimmy Hoffa than a friendly teenager standing behind a fast-food counter. Chances are your five-year-old knows more about the latest electronics than those "knowledgeable" salespeople at the mall.

As much as I bemoan bad customer disservice I celebrate good customer service. It's so rare that it should be applauded and the purveyor of said good customer service should be rewarded for actually delivering satisfaction to the customer above and beyond the call of duty.

So let me tell you the story of my new hero, Ken. I first met Ken when I went into the electronics store where he works to buy a mixing board for my business that records audio products for the Web. In a nutshell, you plug microphones into the mixing board, then connect it to the computer and you can record audio directly to digital format. Totally beside the point of this tale, but I didn't want you thinking that I was purchasing nonmanly cooking utensils.

When I got the mixer installed it didn't work. So I boxed it up and headed back to the store to return it. When I told Ken my problem he didn't just grunt and give me my money back as so many bad customer service reps would do. Instead he asked, "Do you mind if I try it?"

"Knock yourself out," was my reply, confident that if I couldn't get it to work, neither could Ken. Ken took the mixer out of the box and went about hooking it up to one of the computers on display. He started pulling power cords and cables off the display racks and ripping them open and plugging them in. He tore open a new microphone and an adapter and kept going until he had the mixer hooked up and working. Yes, I said working. It turns out the mixer was fine. I just had the wrong power adapter.

Now let's dissect this. Ken could have just given me my money back and been done with me. Instead he was helpful, knowledgeable, patient, and willing to do just about anything to make that darn mixer work. Granted, his desire to help may have been driven by the same testosterone-laden determination that causes all men to drive around lost for hours before finally stopping to ask for directions, but that's beside the point. As customer service goes, I wouldn't trade Ken for all the pimply-faced teenagers working in all the trendy stores in all the malls of America.

I was so impressed that I not only kept the mixing board, I also bought another $50 worth of products. And the next time I need anything electronic, guess where I will buy it? Even if it costs twice as much, I'll buy it from Ken.

Now here's the moral of the story: If you are a business owner who has a gaggle of teenagers in charge of customer service at your store, you would be better off replacing them with a single Ken.

Or with a bunch of wild monkeys.

At least wild monkeys are fun to watch.

CHAPTER 34

Sometimes You Have to Give Customers the Boot

Just as the customer has the right to expect that he will get his money's worth when doing business with you, you have the right to expect that your customer will not demand things that are beyond the scope of realistic expectations (or the contract).

If a customer orders hamburger, he shouldn't expect it to taste like steak unless you have advertised it as such. If a customer brings you a cotton shirt to launder he should not expect a silk shirt in return. It's when the customer's expectations get out of sync with what should realistically be expected that you will have problems.

We have all had customers who expected far more than was their due: customers who were unreasonable, overly demanding, condescending, hard to please, and sometimes even dishonest in their dealings. When a customer's reasonable expectations become unreasonable demands you must decide whether that customer is doing more harm to your business than good.

So here is the line in the sand between "The customer is always right" and "Sometimes the customer is wrong": If a customer crosses the line from being an asset to being a detriment to your business, you should consider giving that customer the boot.

This is easier said than done if that customer constitutes a large chunk of your revenue, but even then you have to consider what your business might be like if that problem customer was not in the picture.

Would the time you spend dealing with the problem customer be better spent on sales calls that might expand your client base and grow your business? After all, a business that is dependent on one client is a house of cards that could tumble down on a whim.

Would your employees be happier not having to deal with this customer? Would you sleep better nights knowing that you don't have a dozen phone messages from him on your desk every morning?

The easiest way to decide how much trouble a customer is worth is to look at the amount of revenue this customer brings in versus the time and expense of meeting his expectations. If this customer pays you $1,000 a month, but costs you $2,000 in time spent keeping him happy, this customer is actually costing you money. Just a handful of these kinds of customers will put you out of business fast.

For example, I once had a client whose business was worth several thousand dollars a year to my software company's bottom line. However, this client proved to be problematic from the second the contract was signed. He and his employees called our office ten times a day and dominated my tech support team's time with IT problems that were not even related to the service we were contracted to provide. It got so bad that my employees cringed every time the phone rang because they were afraid it was this client calling again.

When the time came to renew this client's contract it wasn't hard for me to decide to give him the boot. I simply did the math. This client had added thousands of dollars to my company's bottom line, but had cost me at least that much in handholding and support, not to mention the mental anguish he had caused my employees. I opted not to renew the contract and politely invited the client to take his business elsewhere.

The perfect customer relationship is win/win, meaning that your customer benefits from your product or service and your company prospers by delivering the product or service. The relationship must be built on mutual respect and honest intention. It is when the relationship becomes win/lose that you must be ready to take action. If the customer thinks he can hold you over a barrel and get more out of you than he has paid for, the relationship and your business suffer for it.

Look, you don't need me to hit you in the head with a stupid stick on this one. You know who your problem customers are and you know that you will eventually have to deal with them. You have to consider the value of every customer in the long run, not just their value today.

Is the customer making demands that are beyond the scope of what should be reasonably expected? If customers constantly demand more than they are entitled to and get angry when you refuse to comply, consider giving them the boot.

Is the customer taking advantage of your good graces? Some customers may mistake your willingness to please for weakness and try to wring more out of your relationship than they should. If customers have a record of trying to take advantage of you and play every angle to get more from you than they deserve, consider giving them the boot.

Is this customer a threat to your reputation? Let's face it; there is nothing more harmful to your reputation than a dissatisfied customer with a big mouth. And it does not matter who is at fault in the disagreement, a disgruntled customer is going to bad-mouth you in the end—especially if he was at fault. If you suspect a customer might be the sort to one day air dirty laundry in public, consider giving him the boot.

Does the customer pay in a timely manner? If you have a customer that is consistently 90 to 120 days late in paying even when your contract clearly outlines your payment terms to be otherwise, it may be indicative of other problems to come. If you feel the client is a payment risk, consider giving him the boot.

What's the best way to avoid a customer booting? The best answer is to have a contract that clearly spells out the specifics of the relationship. The contracts I use in my various businesses clearly define the services to be provided, the cost of those services, and the timeline and terms under which those services will be rendered. If there is a deviation from the contract, we write an addendum that details any changes and their effect on the contract. Do I still have to give some customers the boot? You bet, but not very often. It's hard for a customer to cry foul when everything is there in black and white right above his signature.

What if your business doesn't use contracts? Then hang a poster in your shop or have a hand-out that clearly defines what your customer can expect from your business and then deliver what you promise.

If you have a poster or hand-out that clearly outlines your services, your rates, scheduling, return policy, and so forth, there should be very little that the customer can complain about.

I know, famous last words.

CHAPTER 35

Managing Employees Is a Little Like Herding Cats

One of the toughest challenges many entrepreneurs face involves managing employees. In the beginning we all think that it will be cool to build a big business with lots of employees, but the truth is having employees can be a huge pain in the backside. Imagine running a daycare center with a bunch of 200-pound one-year-olds running amok and you'll have an idea of what it's like to manage employees.

Don't believe me? Here is a letter I got from a reader who was finding out the hard way that having employees is a lot like having a houseful of spastic kids.

Q: I started my small business about a year ago and it's grown steadily. I like having my own business, but I'm having a tough time managing people. I have five employees now and it seems like I spend half my time making sure they are doing what they're supposed to be doing and the other half of my time doing things they didn't get done. Things were much easier when I was a one-man shop. Any suggestions?

A: Ah, welcome to the wonderful world of employee management, the bane of many a business owner's existence. I hope you have a full head of hair now, because depending on how quickly you get a grip on this situation, you could end up bald in a very short time. And if you're starting out bald all you can do is put on a cap and pray that your scalp is strong enough to withstand the stress.

Some business experts will tell you that managing people is an art. Others will tell you that managing people is a skill.

I'm here to tell you that managing people is more like herding cats. Just when you think you have them all going in the same direction, one will run off and you have to go catch it. And by the time you get back with the stray cat the rest of the herd has all gone off in different directions. It's no wonder most entrepreneurs hate cats. They remind us how little control we have over our employees.

The hardest part of employee management is maintaining control over your business while the herd is running wild. If your employees are running the business instead of you, it's a little like the inmates taking over the insane asylum. Crazy things might start to happen, like losing customers and being run out of business.

Here's the bottom line: You either manage your employees or they will manage you; it's simple as that.

The key to managing employees is to hire only the best people, train them well, establish boundaries and expectations, get them emotionally vested in the success of your business, and accept nothing but the best from them.

And when you do find that rare employee who gives you 110 percent you should go out of your way to do nice things for him, like giving bonuses, raises, job security, added responsibility, praise, and a big turkey at Christmas. Finding good employees is hard. Keeping them happy shouldn't be. And by good employees I mean honest, loyal, dedicated, hard-working individuals who will give their all for the good of the business and go above and beyond the call of duty to satisfy the customer.

Finding these people is as hard as . . . well . . . herding cats.

Hard to do, but not impossible. Here are a few tips to help you get a better handle on hiring and managing employees.

Hire only experienced, qualified people with a proven track record of performance. Since your employees are usually the main point of contact with customers, it is vital that you hire only experienced, qualified personnel to represent your business. It's also important that the potential employee have a track record of success in the kind of position he's being hired for.

If it's a sales job, you want to hire someone who has proven that he can sell. If it's servicing copiers you want to hire someone who has proven himself a pro at fixing copiers. Forget hiring rookies and offering on-the-job training when it comes to key personnel. Go with an old pro every time, even if it costs you more to do so. The investment will be returned to you manifold.

Screen every applicant thoroughly. There are lots of screening products on the market now that will help you screen applicants for things like honesty, integrity, ambition, former drug use, past criminal behavior, and so forth. These products range from simple paper forms to fancy web-based applications. Find one that suits your needs and use it on every applicant that comes through the door. You will be amazed at how a good screening program will help you weed out problem employees before they are hired.

Perform drug tests and background checks on key personnel. I beg the pardon of those "right to privacy" do-gooders who tell me that a person's personal life and urine contents are none of my business, but if I'm going to be paying someone's salary every week you can be certain that I will exercise my right to check out that person as far as the letter of the law allows. The U.S. government tells me what I can and can't do when it comes to checking out potential employees, not you. Go save a tree and leave me to run my business.

Always check professional references. This is a huge mistake that many employers make. They ask for references, but never check the quality or legitimacy of the references.

Surveys have shown that most job application references are either bogus or just family and friends who are willing to say how great the applicant is. Forget references from family and friends. Ask for the names of their last three employers, then call to verify the information on the application. By law, past employers are limited as to what they can divulge about the applicant, but if you simply ask, Would you hire this person again given the chance?, you will be amazed at what you can learn. The former employer will either answer immediately that they would rehire the person or there will be a long pause on the other end of the phone. Either way, you have found out what you wanted to know.

Never hire out of desperation. Many employers are more concerned with just filling an open slot than filling it with someone qualified to do the work. You see this mostly in the fast-food, retail, and manufacturing industries where the turnover rate is off the scale and finding good employees is like herding mammals of the feline species (last one, I promise). Never hire someone just because they have a pulse. It will always come back to haunt you.

Use a probationary period to weed out nonperformers. You should inform new hires that you have a 60-day probationary period in which you will regularly assess their attitude and performance. If at the end of the probationary period the employee is not the worker you thought he would be, gracefully have a final review and let him go. Most nonperformers will never reach the end of the 60-day period anyway.

When someone does a good job, reward him for it. Incentives are a great way to improve employee performance. We are all like little kids. If we think we're going to get a new toy (or a bonus) for doing a good job, we are more likely to excel. You should reward good performance and make a very big deal out of the fact that you do. You can do this with stock options or bonus checks or free vacations or whatever.

It is important that all your employees understand that when the company does well, they will do well. As the company grows, so will their paychecks.

While this particular reader had his hands full keeping his employees in line, at least he hadn't personalized the employer/employee relationship like the business owner in the next letter.

Take this as gospel: When your employees become your buddies, you're just asking for trouble, as the reader who sent in the next question discovered too late.

Q: One of my key employees is giving me trouble. He has started showing up late for work and has developed a bad attitude in general. The rest of my employees are complaining since they are having to take up his slack. I've tried talking to him, but he doesn't seem to listen. To make matters worse, he has become one of my best friends since I hired him five years ago, so firing him is out of the question. What can I do?

A: One reason I am so qualified to dispense sage business advice is that I have made just about every business blunder you can imagine. I am like the Evel Knievel of the small business world, if Evel Knievel wrote an advice column on motorcycle safety.

One of the more unpleasant things I've had to do is fire a good friend who was not doing the job I hired him to do. He needed a job and I needed an employee, so I thought I would give him a shot. It turned out to be a match made in business hell.

He took advantage of our friendship by showing up late for work, spending time goofing off instead of working, and making a joke out of my complaints about his behavior. Because of our friendship I defended his actions to my other employees, but after a few weeks I knew I had to show him the door. We're still friends, but certainly not like we were before.

The blunder I made was hiring a friend in the first place. I let emotion (i.e., the desire to help my friend gain employment) get in the way of my business sense. That's what you are doing now, and I hate to be the bearer of bad news, but you are going to have to deal with this situation soon or your entire operation may be affected by the actions of this one person.

The blunder you have made is that you have befriended an employee after you hired him, which is something you should never do. I'm not saying you can't be friendly with your employees, but you have attached a considerable amount of emotional baggage to the employer/employee relationship and the result is the situation you are faced with today.

Friends expect preferential treatment simply because they are your friends. The workplace, however, must be a level playing field for all your employees, friends or not. While employees deserve your respect (if it is earned), giving one employee preferential treatment over another is never a good idea. This is a problem experienced by many business owners and managers who allow themselves to become too close to their employees.

I understand that he has become your friend over the years and you'd rather eat rocks than fire him, but you have to consider how his behavior is impacting your business overall. What effect is he having on employee morale, on work schedules, on customer relations, on time spent fixing his mistakes, and most importantly, on the bottom line?

You have two options: Get him back on track or get him off the payroll, period. That may sound cold and politically incorrect, but those are your only choices. Either way, you must be his employer first and friend second.

In his defense, he may have personal reasons for his performance, but as his employer you are legally limited as to how much prying you can do into his home life. As his friend, however, I expect that you already have a good idea what the problem is. If you can help him return to being a productive member of the team, then do so. If not, wish him well, let him go, and move on.

Here are a few suggestions to help you establish and enforce the boundaries of the employer/employee relationship.

Define the relationship. Keep your seat, Dr. Phil, this won't take long. The employer/employee relationship should be well-defined from the outset and the parameters understood by all parties. Some call it "defining the pecking order" or "establishing the food chain." Whatever colorful term you use, it all boils down to this: You can be their boss or you can be their buddy. You cannot be both.

Don't hire friends or relatives. This rule is certainly bendable if you are the owner of the business and you hire your children to work for you. Chances are your offspring already accept you as the ultimate authority figure and managing them in a business environment is second nature. However, even this situation could have a negative impact on your business as nonrelated employees often expect the boss's son, daughter, or best buddy to work less, make more money, and be treated better than everyone else. Whether that's true or not, nepotism and cronyism can create an underlying tension among the ranks.

Establish and adhere to company policies. It's a good idea to have published policies concerning every aspect of your business, including employee behavior and performance expectations. By its very nature the employer/employee relationship is prone to favoritism. Managers can't help but favor those employees who work harder, longer, and faster, but when it comes to adhering to company policies, there should be no preferential treatment of favored employees. Every employee should receive a copy of your published company policies and sign a form stating that they have read, understand, and agree with the same.

The bottom line: Treat everyone the same. It does not matter if the employee is a vice president or a janitor; everyone in your company should be treated the same when it comes to adhering to published company policies and performance expectations.

While it is true that a vice president may be of more value to the company than a janitor, it is also true that a vice president who is running amok can do far more damage to your company than a janitor who lets a toilet back up every once in awhile (there's an analogy there that I will let you figure out on your own).

It's not personal, it's just business. This is what the movie bad guys say to one another right before the shooting starts.

"Hey, Paulie, it's not personal. It's just business."

BLAM! BLAM!

This is the dating equivalent of saying, "It's not you, it's me."

These kinds of statements are not going to make anyone feel better when they are getting dumped or fired. Just ask any former employee or old girlfriend you've used this line on.

If you have to fire an employee—even a friend—do it by the book in a professional manner.

It won't be easy, but you have to remove the emotion and do what's best for you and your business.

CHAPTER 36

If It Were Easy, Everybody Would Do It

E very entrepreneur that I know has, at one time or other, had what I call "a garbage truck moment."

That's when the pressure of running a business starts getting to you and you begin to question whether the entrepreneurial life is right for you. Your sales are in a slump and your debts are in a pile and your employees are running amok and competitors are breathing down your neck and customers aren't returning your calls and you get that nauseous feeling in the pit of your stomach and shooting pains in your chest and you find yourself longing for the apparent simplicity of driving a garbage truck.

Note to garbage truck drivers: Save your hate mail, boys. I know you work very hard and I totally respect what you do. Without you the world would be a very different, very smelly place, indeed.

Even on the best of days running a business can be incredibly stressful, not to mention overwhelming and exhausting. It's only natural that there will be times when you wonder if you're really cut out to run this race.

Asking yourself the "should I just get a real job" question simply means that your human side is showing. And as a human we have a limited tolerance for things we cannot control. And that's really where the stress of being an entrepreneur comes from. We spend so much time worrying about things we can't control that we ultimately lose control of those things that we could.

Worrying about things you can't control is a waste of brain cells. Sure, we can put forth our best efforts to make things turn out in our favor, but we really can't control the outcome on most of the things that affect our business.

So we worry. And worry breeds stress and stress breeds doubt and doubt breeds the feeling that an 800-pound gorilla is using your chest for a lawn chair. It's only natural that you begin to wonder, "Is this what I really want to do? Do I have what it takes to run my own business?"

Consider the following question that I received from a young entrepreneur who was starting to feel that the stress of being in business was going to do him in.

Q: I started my business about a year ago and everything is going fine. We're growing and making a profit, but the stress of running the business is really starting to get to me. I spend more time worrying than working. Sometimes the pressure is almost more than I can take. I'm starting to think that I'm not cut out to run my own business. Do you have any advice that might help me decide what to do?

A: I'm full of advice, my friend, and it's totally free. Just remember, you get what you pay for and I can't be held legally or morally responsible if my advice somehow lands you behind the counter at McDonalds. I'm not Dr. Phil, for petesake. I'm shorter and have more hair and less money.

Seriously, the first thing you need to do is take a few deep breaths and take comfort in the fact that you are not the first entrepreneur to feel the weight of the business world on your shoulders.

Every businessperson, including yours truly, has felt the way you do at one time or another. For some, it's a feeling that occurs daily; especially when things aren't going as well as we'd like them to. And don't think the stress will magically disappear if your business takes off.

I know people who run multimillion-dollar corporations and

they will tell you that the stress level goes up in proportion to the size of the business. These same people will also tell you they love what they do and would never consider doing anything else.

The difference between these entrepreneurs and you is that they have learned not only to handle stress, but to take stress and transform it into a driving force. They feed off the stress. It fuels their creativity and innovation. Stress challenges them, it makes them think, it makes them innovate; it makes them better entrepreneurs.

I think the real question isn't whether you have what it takes to run a business. The real question is do you have what it takes to handle the stress of running a business. These are two very different questions and the answers depend totally on you.

I remember once complaining about the stress of running my business to an older entrepreneur friend of mine. He waved at me like he was swatting a fly and said, "Son, if it was easy, everybody would do it. Now suck it up and move on."

Suck it up and move on—probably the best business advice I've ever gotten. No fortune cookie was ever so on the money. My mentor's eloquent point was this: Running a business is never easy and always stressful, but that's what makes it so dang exciting.

Running a business is like walking a tightrope . . . backward . . . with your eyes shut . . . and your pants on fire . . . and you have to pee.

Man, sure beats working for a living.

What's happening to you has happened to every entrepreneur at some point, including yours truly. The stress is causing you to doubt not only your decision to start your own business, but your ability to run it, as well. There's no magic bullet for dealing with stress and you certainly can't eliminate it totally, so you must learn to handle it.

I believe the key to handling stress is to first identify the source of the stress, then formulate a plan to deal with it.

Here's what I do. Take a pencil and paper and list all the things that are causing you stress. For each item listed ask yourself: Is there anything I can do about this? Is there anything I can do to change this from being a point of stress to a point of accomplishment?

In other words, is this something I have control over?

Stressing over things you can't control is a total waste of time. Tell yourself that you're burning brain cells in vain and mark that item off your list.

Some people don't have this ability. Some people are just natural-born worriers who are not happy unless they have something to worry about. They revel in worry. They work in worry like a great artist works in oils. Even when things are going great they worry that the sky is about to fall.

If you are a natural-born worrier, nothing I say will help you handle stress. Go take a Valium, put on a Pink Floyd album, and watch a *Teletubbies* marathon. You'll feel better in the morning.

Next, determine if each point of stress is something that has happened in the past, is currently happening, or has not yet—or may never—happen.

If the stress point is the past, there's not much you can do but attempt to rectify the situation causing the stress.

If it's a current problem, formulate a plan to deal with the problem and eliminate the stress it's causing. And if you're stressing over things that may never happen, remember what Mark Twain said: "I am an old man and have known a great many troubles, but most of them never happened." Finally, it's important to remember that working for someone else can be just as stressful as working for yourself.

Sure, you don't have the stress (and responsibility) associated with running a business, but you will have other stresses that can be far worse, like impossible work deadlines, sales quotas you can't meet, a boss that learned his management skills on a chain gang, coworkers who don't pull their own weight, or possible layoffs. Very few things in life are without stress. Just ask any garbage truck driver.

CHAPTER 37

Is Brick and Mortar Dead as a Door Nail?

A good portion of my business is conducted over the Internet and if I had my way about it I'd do business 100 percent online. I love the convenience of the Internet; the immediacy of it; the reach and the flexibility. I can carry on an instant messaging conversation with a vendor in the UK while leading a web conference for a room full of high-powered executives in LA and send an e-mail to my virtual assistant in India, all while wearing just my Sponge Bob boxer shorts and old Elvis t-shirt.

I am a huge fan of the Internet and appreciate full well the positive effects Internet-related technology has had on my business. If you're not using everything the Web has to offer to make your business run faster, smoother, better, your business is suffering for it.

Still, I'm always a little surprised when I hear from folks who think that brick and mortar is dead and starting an online business is the only way to go.

While I'm a big Internet advocate, I don't believe we're quite ready to tear down the malls just yet. And at last report Sam Walton was still resting comfortably in his deeply discounted grave, so I'd say brick and mortar is safe, at least for the next few years.

During the dot-com boom the mantra was "Brick and mortar is

dead!" Then when most of the dot-coms crashed like a fat lady sitting in a cheap lawnchair, the mantra suddenly changed back to "The Internet is dead! Long live brick and mortar!"

In both instances those doing the shouting were dead wrong (and highly annoying). My mantra was, "Kill those idiots chanting mantras," but I digress.

I believe that brick-and-mortar businesses will be with us for many years to come. That's not to say that online selling will not continue to grow and overshadow in-store sales in the coming years. But smart retailers realize the potential—and limitations—of the Internet and are making plans accordingly.

While smart retailers know that the Internet has the potential of opening up new sales channels for them, they also know that not all customers will shop online, at least for another generation or two. Until every man, woman, and child on the planet can operate a computer as easily as a cell phone, there will always be consumers who will not buy online.

Smart retailers also understand that a successful online strategy depends on the mindset of the buying public. They understand that the Internet is not replacing business models: It is changing them. Those that adapt will succeed, those that do not will one day close their doors.

When Amazon.com burst onto the scene with big plans to change the way people buy books, Barnes & Noble did not close their brick-and-mortar stores out of fright. They also did not ignore the trend toward online shopping. Instead they directed resources toward building their own online sales arm to compete in the online marketplace.

Many large retailers that were slow to jump on the online shopping bandwagon are now getting serious about online sales. They are using the Web to launch new product lines and sell things you normally would not find in their stores. Wal-Mart, for example, sells products online that would be too pricy for their retail stores, like $6,000 plasma TVs and expensive sports memorabilia.

Setting up an online shop is also cheaper than ever before. A web store that would have cost hundreds of thousands of dollars just a few years ago can now be built for less than $100. This sucks for me, since the arm of my business that made a killing designing high-end websites in the 1990s is now sucking wind like a Hoover vacuum, but it's good news for businesses on a budget.

Online retailers can also stock more items than brick-and-mortar stores that have only so much shelf space.

As more consumers have access to broadband, you will continue to see a rise in online shopping and a rise in the number of companies setting up online points of sale. The great news for web shoppers is that as more retailers go online consumers will have more choices and find lower prices. Sure, businesses will have to learn to compete on more than just price, but that's a good thing. Maybe they'll improve their customer service, concentrate on the quality of their products, and give their customers a reason to buy other than just what's on the red tag.

In my mind that makes the Internet win/win for everyone.

One thing that will definitely ensure that some brick and mortars never go away is what I call "The Try It On Factor." If you have to try it on or want to see how you look in it before you buy, there will always be a need for brick-and-mortar stores.

For example, I always wear cowboy boots (I have a pointed foot) and I would never buy a pair of cowboy boots without trying them on first, so until some genius comes out with a way for me to hold my big foot up to the computer monitor and get a perfect fit, I will buy my boots only in the store.

I do believe that someday the majority of products will be purchased online. We are already seeing this trend in many industries. DVDs, CDs, videotapes (which will definitely go the way of vinyl records in a couple of years), books, cell phones, televisions, computers, and stereos are all big sellers online. It's also commonplace to buy a car from the comfort of home or even to shop for a house. I know because I've done them both several times.

When debating the death of brick and mortar you must also consider the fact that shopping is a social experience for many consumers (i.e., females), who happen to control the purse strings and make most of the buying decisions for their families.

Case in point: Every year my wife and her mother trek to Birmingham and Atlanta for annual shopping trips; as if the half-dozen malls we have in Huntsville aren't adequate enough to satisfy their buying jones. When I point out that there are perfectly good malls right here in our own backyard, I am told that I'm missing the point. The point of these trips is not to buy anything. The point is to shop, to eat, to hang out, to bond. If a purchase is made, that's just gravy.

Scientific studies on these phenomena have concluded that "It's a girl thing."

For men, shopping is a chore to be dreaded and avoided.

For women, shopping is an experience to be relished and repeated—and the more often the better, or so I'm told.

So until my wife and mother-in-law can get the same satisfaction sitting in front of a computer monitor as they do exploring the malls, there will always be brick and mortar.

Long live Sam Walton.

CHAPTER 38

Moving Your Business to the World Wide Web

Much of the e-mail I get these days is from entrepreneurs who either are adding a website to their existing business or are launching a business that operates totally online. Since I have businesses that operate under both models, I fully endorse their desires, but I find that most of them don't have a clue how to get things going.

The one thing you should understand is this: Building an effective business website, no matter how large or small, begins with definition.

Before the first graphic is drawn or the first line of code is written, you must define the website's budget, purpose, target audience, design, navigation, and content. And when that's all said and done you must define the marketing that will bring visitors to your site.

It sounds easy, but you'd be amazed at how many really bad business websites there are out there. Heck, yours is probably one of them, so listen up. Since 1995 my website design business has been building and rebuilding websites for every kind of business you can imagine: from mom-and-pops to multinationals. We've designed (or redesigned) a couple of hundred websites, and along the way I have come to this conclusion: Most business owners wouldn't know good website design if it slammed into their forehead like a bug smashing into a windshield. And for that reason most business websites do a pitiful job of working for their owners.

What's that, you didn't know your business website should work for you? You think it should just sit on a server somewhere taking up digital space and collecting digital dust?

Wrong. Every website, business or otherwise, must serve a purpose, and that's usually where most websites fall short. They serve no purpose because the website owner never gave much thought to it. It's not the website's fault. A website is inanimate. It's just a series of files with programmatic code and images attached. A website is only what you make of it. The only life a website has is the one given to it by its designer and owner.

If the human element doesn't do a good job of defining the building blocks, the website will serve no purpose and eventually die a digital death. Again, it all starts with definition.

Define the budget. Every website, no matter how large or small, must have a realistic budget, with "realistic" being the key word. I can't tell you how many times I've sat with a potential client as they listed off the eight million cool things they wanted their website to do, only to find out that their budget was just a few hundred dollars. I always feel like saying, "Well, you just wasted three hundred dollars of my time, so here's your bill."

Define the purpose. Every website must have a purpose. Purpose drives everything: the audience, the design, the navigation, the content, and the marketing. I could do an entire chapter on purpose, but suffice it to say that there are five categories of purpose under which most websites fall: the purpose to inform, to educate, to entertain, to generate leads, to sell, or a combination thereof. If you fail to define the purpose of the website, all else is just wasted effort.

Define the target audience. Your target audience refers to that segment of the public that you hope to attract to the site. For example, if you sell shoes, your target audience would be anyone with feet. Taking it a step further, if you sold only women's shoes, your target audience would be women (with feet).

Why is defining your target audience so important? If you have no idea who your audience is, how can you expect to design a website that will appeal to them? That sells to them? That keeps them coming back? Your target audience could be customers, investors, job seekers, information seekers, and so on. Define your target audience, then figure out how to serve them.

Define the design. Website design theory has changed over the last few years, primarily because the search engines now ignore graphic-heavy websites and give preference to those that take a minimalist approach to design.

If you look at some of the big-boy websites like GE, Oracle, Raytheon, HP, and others, you will see that in many cases the only graphic on the homepage is the company's logo. Search engines now give higher preference to websites that offer keyword-rich text over flashy graphics. Don't fight the design trend. You will lose.

Define the navigation. Bad navigation is the number-one reason website visitors abandon a website. Navigation refers to the chain of links the visitor uses to get around your site. If your site has an illogical navigational hierarchy or too few or too many links or is simply impossible to get around, you've got problems.

We live in a microwave society. We stand in front of the microwave tapping our foot and glaring at our watch, wondering why it takes so damn long for a bag of popcorn to pop. Why can't a 3-minute egg be done in 30 seconds? If it takes a visitor more than three clicks to get to any page on your site, your navigation needs improvement.

Define the content. Content refers to the information on your website, be it graphics, text, downloadable items, and so forth. Since the top search engines no longer use HTML meta tag data to index websites, it is vital that your website content be keyword heavy, succinct, and well-written to appeal to the search engine spiders.

Define the build method. Next, who will build the website for you? Will you do it yourself using one of the point-and-click website builders or will you hire the kid next door? Will you hire a freelance designer or a professional firm? Budget usually dictates the build method, but be warned, when it comes to website development, you get what you pay for. Sure, the kid next door will throw up a site for you if you buy him a pizza or make your daughter go to the prom with him, but you will end up a with a website that looks like and performs like it was designed by the kid next door.

Define the marketing. If you build it, will they come? Not on your life, at least not without a good marketing campaign. Your website should become a part of all your marketing efforts, online and off.

Put the website address on your business cards, brochures, letterhead, and all collaterals. Include the address in your ads: print, TV, and radio. If you prefer to do online marketing, figure out where your target audience surfs and advertise there.

If marketing is foreign to you, do yourself a favor and call in an expert. Many businesses fail because they simply do not know how to market their products and services effectively.

This is also the downfall of most business websites.

Of course, building a website is only half of the puzzle. Getting visitors to your website is the tricky part, as every new website owner discovers, often to their dismay. I'm not sure why business owners, who spend thousands on advertising and promotion for their brick-and-mortar store, think that people will flock in droves to their website without equal promotion.

Let's look at a question from Sean on that topic.

Q: I recently launched a website for my sporting goods business and I have not had a single visitor come by. I thought I'd be making sales off the website from day one, but that hasn't been the case. Do I need to do anything special to attract customers to my website? I know nothing about search engines and marketing as such. Please tell me where to begin.

A: That is a question that has been asked by every business person who has ever launched a website. If I build it, will they come? Of course they will—if you've built a website that appeals to dead baseball players.

For those of you who didn't get the *Field of Dreams* reference, let me put it this way: No, Sean, if you build it they will not come, at least not without some effort on your part.

Assuming that a website will automatically attract customers is the single biggest mistake that many business owners make. It is this mistake that eventually leads them to dismiss their website as a failure and abandon their online sales efforts.

I can't tell you how many times I've heard a client say, "Well, I threw up a website, but nobody ever came to it and I didn't sell a single thing from it! Dang thing was a waste of time, if you ask me."

Forgive me, but "threw up" is the operative term there. These short-sighted entrepreneurs (God bless them) mistakenly think that all they have to do is throw up a website and then their business will automatically double overnight. And when nothing happens they blame it on the infallibility of the Internet, on El Nino, on the Bossa Nova, on their customers . . . everything but their own lack of marketing efforts.

If you build it, will they come? That, Sean, depends totally on you.

When it comes to attracting customers, opening an online business (or an online branch of an existing business) is no different from opening a traditional brick-and-mortar shop. Without a little fanfare and a well-devised marketing plan, chances are your website will become just another spot of roadkill on the information superhighway.

The first step in devising your marketing plan is to ask yourself this question: Who is my customer? Who is it that I want to attract to my website? Believe it or not, this is a question many entrepreneurs fail to ask. The identity of your customer is incredibly important because if you don't know who your customers are, how can you expect to market to them?

The next question concerns the locality of your customer. Do you want to attract a local or global clientele to your website? If the answer is local, then you will gear your marketing efforts toward customers in your own backyard, which means incorporating your website launch with your offline marketing efforts.

If the website is the online branch of a brick-and-mortar business, include the website URL in all your print materials and advertising campaigns. Consider running ads in the local paper, on radio or TV, announcing the launch of your site. Use direct mail or in-store posters to announce the site launch to your existing customer base. In short, keep doing what you're doing to attract customers to your physical store, just add your website address to the mix.

Just remember, it's important to consider your website a branch of your brick-and-mortar business because that's exactly what it is. A good business website will help you sell more products, widen your range of clientele, and increase your revenue without adding overhead. Don't sell your website short. Make it work for you.

If you are seeking a global audience, your marketing efforts will be quite different. Attracting customers from around the world is a more difficult task than attracting customers from around the block. Fortunately, the task is not impossible. The Internet has leveled the playing field in many ways. Now every business, no matter how large or small, has the ability to do business internationally.

In the most basic sense, an online marketing campaign to attract global customers should include the following efforts.

Register with search engines. There's not enough room in this chapter for a thorough discussion of search engines and their effectiveness (or lack thereof) in driving traffic to a website. Suffice it to say that 95 percent of search engine traffic comes from Google and Yahoo!, so start there. It's also important to realize that just registering with search engines does not guarantee you traffic, but it certainly can't hurt.

Unfortunately, the free search engine lunch ran out a couple of years ago when search engines figured out that people would actually pay for listings and higher placement. Since that time the only way to guarantee a high (or at least higher than others) ranking is to pay for it.

Both Yahoo! and Google have "pay-per-click" advertising programs that can get your business high in the paid rankings. Visit their respective websites for details on these programs. Be prepared to spend several hundred dollars at a minimum to get started. I recommend finding a Search Engine Optimization (SEO) service to manage your search engine advertising efforts for you. Effective SEO requires time, expertise, and constant tweaking and testing. And if you're like most entrepreneurs, patience is not one of your strong suits, so trying to figure out pay-per-click advertising will be about as much fun as doing calculus with your toes.

Exchange links with similar sites. One free way to drive customers to your website is through link exchanges with sites of similar interest. Chances are you won't get a lot of traffic, but it's free and you get what you pay for.

Locate sites that make a good match to your own and contact the owner to ask if they will link to your site in exchange for you linking to theirs. If you sell golf balls on your website, set up a link exchange with another website that sells golf clubs. You post a link to them and they post a link to you. It's called digital back scratching, and if done properly, can work well to drive traffic your way. As with SEO there are lots of services that can help you get started with link exchanges. Do a Google search to find reputable link exchange companies and make sure you ask for references as many of them will make claims they can't back up.

Go to where the customers are. If the mountain won't come to Mohammed, then Mohammed must go to the mountain. One little-known way to attract customers to your website is to market your products on a mega-site like eBay. There are thousands and thousands of people on eBay at any given time and each one is potentially your customer, so it's a great place to drum up business.

Your goal is not to make a living selling on eBay, but to use eBay as a marketing tool to drive traffic back to your business website. This is called filling your funnel. Go to where the customers are, then bring them back home with you.

Let's use our golf ball example. Post a few auctions on eBay selling your golf balls at a ridiculously low price so your auction attracts plenty of attention. When customers make a purchase, add them to your client list and send them an e-mail inviting them to visit your website for more great products. eBay also lets you create your own "About Me" page that you can use to advertise your business. To learn more visit ebay.com.

We have just scratched the surface, but I hope this is enough to get you started. I wish I could tell you that attracting customers to your website is easy, but the truth is, it's anything but.

It takes hard work, creativity, and above all, perseverance.

When it comes to the World Wide Web, size really doesn't matter. It's my belief that every business should have a website, no matter how large or small you may be. The next question from Robin L. addresses that topic.

Q: My business is very small, just me and two employees, and our product really can't be sold online. Do I really need a website?

A: Congratulations, you are the one-millionth person to ask me that question. Smile for the cameras, brush the streamers and confetti from your hair and listen closely, because I'm about to answer for the millionth time what has become one of the most important and often-asked questions of the digital business age.

Before I answer, however, let's flash back to the very first time I was asked this question. It was circa 1998, during the toddler years of the Internet, just after Al Gore laid claim to having given birth to the concept a few short years before.

I was giving a speech on the impact of the Internet on small business at an association luncheon in Montgomery, Alabama. My motto then was: Feed me and I will speak. I have the same motto today, but I now expect dessert to be included in exchange for the sharing of my vast wisdom.

In 1998, which was decades ago in Internet years, the future of electronic commerce, or "e-commerce" as it's come to be known, was anybody's guess, but even the most negative futurists agreed that all the signs indicated that a large portion of future business revenues would be derived from online transactions, or from offline transactions that were the result of online marketing efforts.

So, should your business have a website, even if your business is small and sells products or services that you don't think can be sold online? My answer in 1998 is the same as my answer today: Yes, if you have a business, you should have a website. Period. Thank you, drive through. Now serving customer number one million and one.

Also, don't be so quick to dismiss your product as one that can't be sold online. Nowadays there is very little that cannot be sold over the Internet. More than 20 million shoppers are now online, purchasing everything from books to computers to cars to real estate to jet airplanes to natural gas to you name it. If you can imagine it, someone will figure out how to sell it online.

Let me clarify one point: I am not saying that you should put all your efforts into selling your wares over the Internet, though if your product lends itself to easy online sales, you certainly should be considering it.

The point to be made here is that you should at the very least have a presence on the World Wide Web so that customers, potential employees, business partners, and perhaps even investors can quickly and easily find out more about your business and the products or services you have to offer.

That said, it's not enough that you just have a website. You must have a professional-looking website if you want to be taken seriously. Since many consumers now search for information online prior to making a purchase at a brick-and-mortar store, your website may be the first chance you have at making a good impression on a potential buyer. If your website looks like it was designed by a barrel of colorblind monkeys, your chance at making a good first impression will be lost.

One of the great things about the Internet is that it has leveled the playing field when it comes to competing with the big boys. As mentioned, you have one shot at making a good first impression and, with a well-designed website, your little operation can project the image and professionalism of a much larger company.

The inverse is also true. I've seen many big company websites that were so badly designed and hard to navigate that they completely lacked professionalism and credibility. Good for you, too bad for them.

You also mention that yours is a small operation, but when it comes to benefiting from a website, size does not matter. I don't care if you are a one-man show or a ten-thousand-employee corporate giant; if you do not have a website you are losing business to other companies that do.

CHAPTER 39

Can You Really Make Money with an Online Business?

One thing that I've noticed about the Internet Age is the perception by many folks that making money online is easier than making money off. That is true to a degree. It's easier to open a web store than a corner store. It's faster and cheaper to develop a digital product than a manufactured one. It is possible to make massive amounts of money in a very short period of time selling nothing more than ideas and electrons. Still, that does not mean that you can build a website, snap your fingers, and watch the money flow like honey.

While the Internet does afford many shortcuts and opens up many opportunities, it still does not offer the "get rich quick" solution that many are searching for. Internet marketing is a business, and must be approached as such. There are shortcuts, but there are no "easy" buttons.

Consider the following:

Q: Tim, I have spent the past few months trying to start my own Internet marketing business, but I'm getting nowhere. I'm getting really frustrated because it's just not happening as fast as I thought it would. According to my research you're the Dr. Phil of Internet marketing, so tell me, how can somebody with no technical skills but lots of persistence succeed with an online business, and do so quickly?

A: The Dr. Phil of Internet marketing? I don't know about that, but I'd gladly trade some of my hair for some of his money.

First, let me say that I understand your frustration, but it has been my experience that people in your situation create much of their own frustration because they expect results overnight. This is the Internet, they say, everything happens quickly on the Internet! I'll start a business today and be rich by Friday! Yeah, right.

While the Internet does move quickly, it usually leaves such naive thinkers standing in the dust wondering why their online business failed. The reason this happens so often is the person didn't take the time to learn about the Internet marketing industry before taking the entrepreneurial leap.

Starting an Internet business and getting it profitable quickly is easy for me now, but my first year as an online entrepreneur was a total disaster. I wasted thousands of dollars and hundreds of hours on dozens of ventures that ended in failure. Then one day it hit me: Succeeding as an Internet marketer would be much easier if I knew what the heck I was doing.

I, like so many others before me and so many others since, didn't take the time to educate myself on the nuts and bolts of the Internet marketing industry. I saw others making money online and figured if they could do it, I could, too. I found the crowded pool and dove in head first. I almost drowned because I had not taken the time to learn how to swim. Heck, I couldn't even float.

So I stopped everything I was doing and became a student instead of a practitioner. I discovered that I was making every mistake in the book because I had not taken the time to read the book. I didn't know what to do and, more importantly, what not to do.

Lightbulbs slowly kicked on and today the online arm of my business generates ten times the revenue of my brick-and-mortar ventures, but it took my stepping back and reassessing my entire thinking to ultimately learn how to succeed as an online entrepreneur. And I succeeded in baby steps, not giant leaps. There were no home runs at first. There were a lot of foul balls and finally lots of base hits. That's how you succeed online.

Here's my advice for anyone considering an Internet marketing business:

There is no such thing as a real get-rich-quick opportunity. If someone tells you that you can start with no money and no experience and make hundreds of thousands of dollars overnight they are lying to you and you are a fool for believing them. Yes, you can make lots of money in a short period of time as an Internet marketer, but you're not going to get rich this week unless you hit the lottery or your rich uncle dies. Be realistic, be smart, be logical. If it sounds too good to be true, it is.

Starting an Internet business is much like starting a brick-and-mortar business. Both take hard work, dedication, perseverance, a little luck, and an investment of time and money. Just because your business is "virtual" doesn't mean that you don't have to put in the time and effort to get things going.

You must have patience and realistic expectations. The problem with us humans is that we are an impatient species. We are a microwave society in which nothing happens fast enough. In business, very little happens quickly. Until you understand that, you will drive yourself to failure every time. You will start ventures and quickly abandon them. You will grow frustrated and you will fail.

Learn before you leap. If technical ability was a prerequisite for Internet marketing success, 99 percent of the so-called Internet big dogs (this pup included) would be back working a day job. You can hire someone to write an e-book or hack together a piece of software for you, but finding someone to do your thinking for you is hard. Trust me, I know.

Finally, remember this: Large-scale success—whether online or off—is built upon a foundation of many small successes, and laying that foundation requires knowledge and time.

CHAPTER 40

The Last Word (For Now)

We've covered a lot of ground in this book: some of it muddy; some covered with dew and nice green grass; and some of it strewn with nice tidy piles of BS. No matter what you now have stuck to the bottom of your shoes, I hope you can appreciate the intent of the gardener who helped put it there.

My goal here was to entertain and enlighten you, to make you laugh, to make you think, and perhaps even to make you a little mad.

I wanted to make you look inward and outward and all around.

If I have accomplished only one of those feats . . . well, I haven't done my job very well and perhaps you'd be better off reading Harry Potter.

The moral of this story is this: You can do anything you want to do; you can be anything you want to be; you can climb the highest mountains and swim the deepest rivers.

All you need is a dream, a plan, and the get-up-and-go to pry your backside off the couch and make it happen.

As Mama would say, "Be careful what you wish (and work) for. You just might get it."

For More Information on Tim Knox Products and Services

Tim Knox Official Website
Tim's official website is one of the highest-ranked, fastest-growing small business websites on the World Wide Web. TimKnox.com is packed with free and paid content that can help you successfully start, build, and manage your own small or big business.

- http://www.timknox.com

Small Business Q&A with Tim Knox
Given his skill at mixing commonsense business advice with knee-slapping humor, it's no surprise that Tim's syndicated newspaper column is one of the most popular small business features in print and on the Web. Tim's columns are available for syndication and reprint. You can also access all of Tim's columns via his website at:

- http://www.timknox.com/columns.php

The Tim Knox Radio Show
Tim hosts two weekly radio shows and a monthly Internet podcast that you can listen to live or streamed via the Web. Weekly replays of all shows are also available. For more information or to listen now, visit:

- http://www.timknox.com/ontheair.php

Invite Tim to Speak to Your Organization

To hear most so-called experts tell it, you need PhD, MBA, or some other combination of letters after your name to be successful, but Tim has proven that just isn't true. In Tim's keynote your audience will find much more than funny stories and keen insights about business: They'll find real-world advice based on Tim's own successful career as a corporate executive, entrepreneur, and business leader. What can your organization learn from Tim and his Mama? Contact Tim to find out.

- http://www.timknox.com/speaking.php

Personal Coaching

Tim is available on a limited basis to provide private telephone and in-person coaching to entrepreneurs and executives. Due to the demands on his time Tim works with only a handful of clients a month. For more information, visit:

- http://www.timknox.com/mentoring.php

The Tim Knox Newsletter

The Tim Knox Newsletter is delivered every week to over 65,000 subscribers and is one of the Web's most popular business information resources. To preview Tim's newsletter and subscribe free, visit:

- http://www.timknox.com/newsletter.php

Tim's Humor Site: The Voices in My Head

Tim's award-winning humor site, The Voices in My Head, which features his critically acclaimed humor column and hilarious cartoons, is guaranteed to make you laugh and think at the same time. Visit:

- http://humor.timknox.com